1953

M

VICTORS' JUSTICE

The Humanist Library

X

THE HUMANIST LIBRARY
VICTORS' JUSTICE

A Letter Intended to Have Been Sent
To a Friend Recently in Germany

by

Montgomery Belgion

Ev'n victors are by victories undone.
Dryden

HENRY REGNERY COMPANY
Hinsdale, Illinois

1949

NOTE

I HAVE NO DIFFICULTY IN HOLDING STRONG
opinions. Some I have held longer than I realize. I have
imagined that I was expressing one for the first time, and
then have happened to discover that I had only forgotten
having expressed it years before. The opinions supported
in the following pages I already avowed in 1938. My
difficulty is not in holding opinions. My difficulty lies in
ascertaining why I hold the particular opinions I do.

In February 1947 I published in England a little book
called *Epitaph on Nuremberg*. It was written between
October 1945 and August 1946, at a time, that is to say,
when much germane information had not yet become
public. A publisher having lately proposed to issue the
book in the United States, it occurred to both of us
that the opportunity ought to be taken of expanding it.
In the process of adding, however, I have been led to
rewrite; not because my opinions have changed since
1946, any more than they have since 1938, but because
I have discovered for them reasons which were not then
apparent to me. This is virtually a new book.

I have had the benefit of reading publications by Dr. H. A. Smith, till 1946 professor of international law in the University of London, and by Mr. Louis Le Fur, formerly professor of law at Paris; and also the text of a lecture delivered at Heidelberg in 1947 by Professor Eduard Wahl. I wish also to acknowledge little helpful acts of kindness by Mr. Peter Baker, Mr. Felix Morley, and Mr. Henry Regnery, and valuable textual suggestions from Mr. Philip N. Starbuck.

But of course for everything I say in the following pages I alone am responsible.

M. B.

July 1948.

VICTORS' JUSTICE

My dear Daniel,

At the end of 1945 you were posted to duty in occupied Germany. You had already passed the greater part of the war in that country. In the spring of 1941 you and I were among the British and Yugoslav troops who, after retreating to the shores of the Peloponnesus, were made captive by the enemy. I was repatriated in 1944. You remained a prisoner to the end. It was an American army that delivered you. Before the Americans had you flown home, you were able to take the measure of their mood. You observed that in the invasion of Germany they believed themselves to be conducting a punitive expedition such as the early transatlantic settlers had often undertaken against the Redskins. In that interpretation of the nature of their task the Americans were not singular. All the invaders went forward into Germany animated by the same spirit. The Germans were not simply an enemy; they were a kind of rebel who had to be subdued.

Having been brought to surrender, the Germans were denied any longer a government of their own, and their conquerors settled down among them to hold them in indefinite subjection. But whatever the animus of the Russians and the French, Germany was not treated in that way by the British and the Americans solely for the sake of material gain. The object avowed by the latter was repression. So was it that of the French. Upon your return as a very minor overlord to the scene of your previous detention, you found, in the area in British occupation, that everything was being done as if it were the sequel to quelling disorder, and so it was in the other areas of the country. In the high summer of 1945, the four chieftains of the victorious peoples had gone together into the recesses of Potsdam Park as into a cloud and had re-emerged bearing in their hands, like new tables of Sinai, a set of commandments to the vanquished. The regimen so codified was not to be imposed on the native inhabitants of any particular region alone, but on all Germans, and its ostensible purpose was systematic retribution. Occupation, summary annexations of territory, deportations from east to west, the levy of reparations, the depression of the standard of living—all that had been decreed as the infliction of a penalty.

I do not expect my words to be translated into Russian, and they are meant to apply only to the attitude and conduct of the three victorious powers of the West. If those powers had the feeling that they were being policemen, colonial soldiery, or schoolmasters, that they had been called upon to restore order and to punish disturbers of the peace, they did not attribute the feeling to their possession of superior strength or to the heat of triumph and wrath. They believed they had a warrant. And the warrant was the 'war guilt' of the vanquished. The western victors professed to have a title to act as they were doing, a warrant both for the kind of victory

2

on which they insisted and for the kind of provisional peace which they afterwards decreed. The title and the warrant came from the assertion that, if there had been war, the vanquished, and the vanquished alone, were responsible. The Germans were to be understood not only to have suffered defeat, but also to bear the blame for the trouble to which the victors had been put in defeating them.

Moreover, the blame was to be considered all the greater that the Germans had been represented as having conducted the war on their side entirely without scruple, and, among other enormities, as having enslaved and murdered many thousands of the peoples whom they were supposed to have gratuitously attacked. On the side ultimately victorious certain assumptions had been adopted from the beginning. It was, for instance, assumed in high quarters that the will to victory could only be kept hot in the mass of the combatant peoples if steadily subjected to the fires of hate. On the Continent especially, the actions of the enemy played into the hands of the leaders who had made this assumption, so that to fan the fires of hate became child's play. Hence in the hour of victory the triumphant peoples were almost unanimous in regarding the Germans as guilty twice over, as having not only begun the war, but also as having made it needlessly cruel.

The nature of this particular title and the character of the after-war conduct towards the defeated which it was held to justify were not unconnected. Indeed, the connexion was unmistakable. Everything on which the three western victors insisted was a form of punishment, and punishment was needful because the Germans had been guilty. For instance, if there had to be reparations, it was on the ground that damage, wilful and unnecessary, had been inflicted. In the autumn of 1947 a petition signed by two thousand prominent English men and

3

women was delivered to Mr. Attlee, the British prime minister, begging him to end the detention of German prisoners of war both in England and in the British possessions. The petition Mr. Attlee rejected, and the principal reason which he gave for rejecting it was that German prisoners of war, by means of their labour, were making one form of reparation for German aggression. The connexion between the title of the victors to adopt their policy and the character of that policy itself could not have been asserted more clearly.

But although the western victors produced a warrant for their policy, that policy was not successful. From the first, and especially in England and the United States, the details of the retribution to Germany specified in the Potsdam declaration gave rise to far-reaching criticisms, and, so far as the British and American authorities were concerned, the attempt to carry out retribution in that form very quickly showed the policy to be unworkable. It had to be modified. Its rigours even the French were driven by 1947 to attenuate. It is true that, as criticism was confined to details, so details alone came to be modified. The principle itself, that, as the Germans had been guilty they deserved to be punished—that was never questioned. Notably, the legitimacy of levying reparations was not doubted. Yet events soon engendered the suspicion that more than details had been wrong. The British and American authorities came to co-operate more closely together, and their views seemed, broadly speaking, to harmonize. But the rumble of disagreement between them and the French authorities grew too loud to be successfully muffled. Further, far more radical differences of opinion regarding the operation of policy led to more serious discord between the three western victors in unison and their former great ally in the East.

Nor was that all. In effect, the western victors had argued as follows. As Germany alone had been respon-

4

sible for the outbreak of war, let the Germans be punished, and war in the future would be avoided. The western victors confined themselves to taking measures for meting out retribution to the vanquished, but they claimed that in this they were doing what was best in behalf of peace, and that the peace of Europe and of the world was alone what they had at heart. The most certain means of promoting peace for the future was, they said, to punish those who had broken it in the past.

In 1945 the argument was accepted by the public at its face value, but within a few years afterwards it seemed odd, if true, that as a result of the behaviour of the western victors the safety of the peace of Europe and of the world should only be more precarious than ever.

And further, already once before in this century it had been asserted at the end of a great war by one side—the victorious side—that the other side—the defeated side—had alone been to blame for its outbreak. Already once before the victors had heaped retribution on the vanquished, invoking as their title to do so that same assertion, that the vanquished alone were guilty, and, far from promoting peace, their conduct had led to a diametrically opposite consequence. Whatever the rights and wrongs of the matter, there is no denying, (a) that in 1919 the rulers of France, Britain, and the United States were masters of the world, and could have reshaped it as they would; and (b) that twenty years after, Europe was again at war.

From this previous experience it was possible to draw any one of three conclusions.

A first conclusion was that, even if it were possible for one side alone in a war to be responsible for its outbreak, nothing was to be gained by the punishment of that side, when defeated, by the other and triumphant side, and that in fact for the winning side in a war to punish the losing side does not assist the security of peace.

5

A second possible conclusion was that the assertion after a war of the 'war guilt' of the vanquished is misleading and dangerous, and serves but to disguise from the victors and their public the real sources of international disturbance.

The third and last possible conclusion was that the means of retribution which the victors decided in 1919 to take against the vanquished were not sufficiently severe, and that that was why war came again.

Of those three possible conclusions the western victors of 1945 were content to draw only the last. Was that to display the enlightenment associated with Grahamstown, Canford, or Groton, or was it to betray the unimaginative atrabiliousness of Mr. Squeers?

Article 231 of the Treaty of Versailles was as follows:

The allied and associated governments affirm, and Germany accepts, the responsibility of Germany and her allies for causing all the loss and damage to which the allied and associated governments and their nationals have been subjected as a consequence of the war imposed upon them by the aggression of Germany and her allies.

With regard to the presence in this clause of the words 'Germany accepts', it should be remembered that the German plenipotentiaries were not allowed to discuss the treaty, and simply had it presented to them for signature. They protested against the inclusion of the article, and of the four articles preceding it, but their protests were ignored. The way was thus left open for German writers presently to declare that the responsibility for damage asserted in the treaty had not in fact been accepted by the vanquished. During the next decade after 1919, Article 231 of the treaty gave rise in Germany to a vast literature, and the accusation—interpreted as one of exclusive 'war guilt'—went on being indignantly disputed there. All the way to 1939, and indeed still later, the

6

German National Socialist party was vociferous in rejecting the accusation, and even went the length of contending, albeit with feeble sophistry, that in 1918 Germany had not really been defeated. The western invaders of Germany in 1945 were evidently resolved that that was not to be allowed to happen again.

The punishment decided upon in 1919 had not been sufficiently severe. That this was the only conclusion drawn from the fact that war had broken out again is shown by the tenour of a message which Field-Marshal Montgomery broadcast in June 1945 to Germans of the area of the country in British occupation. He then said:[1]

This time the allies were determined that you should learn your lesson; not only that you have been defeated, which you must know by now, but that you—your nation—were again guilty of beginning a war. . . .

In the war of 1914, which was started by your leaders, your armed forces were beaten in the field. Your generals surrendered and in the Treaty of Versailles your leaders admitted that Germany was responsible for the war. The capitulation, however, took place in France. Hostilities did not take place on German soil. This led your leaders to spread the fairy tale that your armed forces had never been defeated, and later on they repudiated the war guilt paragraph of the Treaty of Versailles.

Thus it was that this second time the western armies invaded Germany and did not pause in their advance till they had received the unconditional surrender of the enemy. Thus it was that Germany was not allowed any longer to have a government of her own, and that the victors settled down in occupation of the country. Thus it was that the whole punitive regimen devised and decreed at Potsdam was so much more draconian than any measures taken after 1918.

And as it was felt that the punishment had only to be

[1] *The Times* (London), 11 June 1945.

7

more severe and it would be effective, so it was imagined that the 'war guilt' of the vanquished—the assertion of which constituted, I repeat, the warrant for the punishment—could be established unmistakably. In 1919 the 'war guilt' had been merely asserted in the peace treaty. Ten years later, in an article contributed to the *Encyclopaedia Britannica*,[1] the late J. L. Garvin was moved to declare:

From the standpoint of the characteristic thought of the English people Article 231 of the Treaty of Versailles [the 'war guilt' clause] has no moral weight and no judicial validity. . . . To speak of 'guilt' in connexion with the rival forces, inspired by irreconcilable ideas of justification, is an extreme triviality. . . . Article 231 is already a dead letter in the moral sense.

Cause for a statement of that kind—that too was not to be allowed again. Now, instead of a mere assertion in a treaty, there would be a trial of the former German leaders, they would be pronounced guilty by a court, and it was thought that this pronouncement would provide, for the meting out of retribution, a warrant beyond challenge.

In the conduct of the war of 1914 the Germans had often given little heed to the laws and usages of war which, as the result of conferences at The Hague towards the end of the nineteenth century and again at the beginning of the twentieth, a majority of civilized nations had agreed to respect. When the first exchange of sick and wounded prisoners of war took place, the English prisoners who were being repatriated brought with them a list of specific accusations against their captors. The unrestricted submarine warfare which the German navy waged in retaliation for the British blockade helped to

[1] *Encyclopaedia Britannica*, 14th ed.

8

spread a belief in German ruthlessness and German 'frightfulness'. In the second war the German army in the field behaved much better—at least in the West in 1940. But as the war dragged on, and again German submarines strove to counteract the effects of blockade, and the Germans had so wide a territory to police and to guard, and resistance movements became active in the countries in German occupation, and the German war effort needed more and more labour, excesses inevitably occurred, and there were acts of repressive savagery. In 1942 the British and United States governments made a joint delaration. The delivery into allied hands of so-called 'war criminals' among the vanquished would be, they stated, a condition of the armistice. A year later, at a meeting in London of the representatives of seventeen countries, a War Crimes Commission was formed. From the beginning it seems to have been intended, in the event of victory, to put the German leaders on trial as well as the actual persons alleged to have been responsible for ordering or committing so-called 'war crimes'. But later, at the request of the United States government, the scope of the intended trial of the leaders was widened. It was decided that they should be tried, not only on a charge of general responsibility for alleged 'war crimes', but also on three other charges—a charge of responsibility for 'crimes against humanity', a charge of having formed 'a common plan or conspiracy' to wage 'aggressive war', and a charge of responsibility for 'crimes against peace'. It must have been thought that the return by the court of a verdict of guilty as regards the two latter charges—'conspiracy to wage aggressive war' and 'crimes against peace'—would be an act establishing German 'war guilt' in a manner which, unlike the insertion of a 'war guilt' clause in the Treaty of Versailles, could not be disputed.

9

In some quarters, furthermore, there was unquestionably expressed the hope that the condemnation and sentence of the German leaders on a charge of having resorted to 'aggressive war' would have another value. Britain and the United States stoutly professed the wish to safeguard peace from again being disturbed. It was thought that the condemnation and sentence of the German leaders would be in accordance with that wish. Not only would the tribunal's verdict provide the western victors with a strong title to mete out retribution to the vanquished, but also the trial and sentences might perhaps point the way to a general acceptance of the ruling that to go to war was an 'international crime'. Already there had been established at The Hague an international court of arbitration, and the newly formed United Nations Organization was to include—in succession to the court at The Hague—a new court with the same functions. Why not an international court of criminal justice as well? If the formation of an international police force was still a dream, at least here was an occasion on which eighteen civilized countries (i.e. the seventeen countries of the war crimes commission, plus Russia, which was not represented on the commission) were deputing four of their number to act as policemen. If only it were generally admitted that to resort to war was a crime, then a subsequent devising of procedure, courts, and punishment would be perfectly proper. That was how the range of law had grown and expanded in the past. As the burglar or murderer is arrested, tried, and sentenced inside a particular country, so here war-makers (who were, after all, far greater criminals than burglars or single murderers) would be handed over to justice. The result could only be that international law would be given sanctions or penalties for its enforcement. An ordered system of justice between state and state might come to be instituted. Such expectations in the effect of the trial were summed up, before it began, in one sentence of an editorial article in *The Times*. The newspaper prognosticated that[1]

The decision may become a precedent upon which jurists of the future can found an international criminal system.

The Trial of the former German leaders took place. It opened on 20 November 1945 and ended on 1 October 1946. As it drew towards its close, in the summer of 1946, the chief proscutor for the British government, Sir Hartley Shawcross, then attorney-general, put forward the same hope in his final speech, in which he said:[2]

On the fate of these men [the men in the dock] great issues must still depend. For the ways of truth and righteousness between the nations of the world, the hope of future international co-operation in the administration of law and justice, are in your hands.

Such expectations and hopes were very fine, even if they exhibited confusion of thought. But there were other possibilities, and they too deserved consideration. For one thing, as I have said, the assertion of the 'war guilt' of the vanquished in 1919 did not prevent another war. The after-war conduct of the victors in the years following 1919—a conduct for which they took the warrant from the assertion—had as its only unmistakable consequence that in 1939 Europe again became a battleground. What if, from the fact that the settlement imposed in 1919 had not prevented a return of war, the victors of 1945 had drawn a mistaken conclusion? As I have said, that conclusion was that the punishment of the vanquished after 1918 had not resulted in the preservation of peace simply because it had not been sufficiently severe. But

[1] *The Times* (London), 19 October 1945.
[2] *The Times* (London), 29 July 1946.

from that failure other conclusions might have been drawn. I have propounded them. It might have been concluded that nothing is gained by the punishment after a war of the defeated side by the winning side, and that in fact for the winning side in a war to punish the losing side does not ensure the security of peace. It might have been concluded that the assertion after a war of exclusive 'war guilt' of the vanquished is misleading and dangerous, and serves but to disguise from the victors and their public the real sources of international disturbance. What if either or both those conclusions were the true conclusions to be drawn from the story of the twenty years after 1919?

Again, supposing the high hopes of an expansion and fortifying of international law and of the setting up of an ordered system of justice between state and state were visionary, that the very nature of international law made such hopes vain, and supposing that the verdict rendered at such a trial could not be beyond dispute? Supposing that, like the 'war guilt' clause of the Treaty of Versailles, the verdict became a subject of interminable discussion and complaint? What then? What, for instance, of the claims of the western victors to reparations? After 1945 the warrant for that claim was the assertion of exclusive 'war guilt' made in the Judgement of the tribunal. 'The tribunal has decided that certain of the defendants planned and waged aggressive wars against twelve nations, and were therefore guilty of this series of crimes.' If the trial itself proved to deserve that very discredit and condemnation that were heaped on the German leaders, then the basis of the claim to reparations would be gone and that claim would in turn lose its justice.

The world had been led to believe that the claims of the victors to reparations in 1919 were based on the assertion of German 'war guilt'. Recently, we have been told, however, that the opposite was true, and that it was for the sake of reparations that the Germans were saddled with the guilt of having caused the war of 1914. The late Etienne Mantoux was the son of the official interpreter at the Paris peace conference of 1919. He may be considered to have been in a position to learn what went on. He left behind at his death a book which has duly been published. It is entirely about the Treaty of Versailles, and his concern in it was to justify the French share in the drafting and enforcing of the instrument. His concern led him to a curious admission. The presence of Article 231 in the treaty is to be attributed, he says, to the ingenuity in compromise of the American delegation. President Wilson's note to the German government on 5 November 1918 had held out the promise of 'a just and honourable peace'. The American delegation at Paris considered that in view of this promise it was impossible for a treaty to which the United States was being a party to contain an unmotivated demand that Germany should make reparations to the victors. Indeed, President Wilson himself cabled from Washington that the United States government was bound in honour to refuse to join in such a demand. Yet the French government was clamorous for reparations to be exacted, and the British delegation had been committed by the assurance given publicly in England by Lloyd George, the prime minister, that 'Germany would be squeezed till the pips squeaked'. So the American delegation, according to Etienne Mantoux, hit on a solution which was thought to reconcile British and French requirements with Wilsonian scruples. If Germany were saddled with 'war guilt' and asserted to have committed 'aggression', the insistence on reparations would become legitimate. So it was that the text of Article No. 231 was drafted.[1]

[1] *The Carthaginian Peace* (1946), p. 100.

Germany had to be guilty of having caused the war for the sake of reparations.

As the end of the second war approached, and with it the decisive triumph of the same allies, there was raised again a cry for reparations. In 1919 the amount which Germany was to pay had been put, especially by the French, in astronomical figures. In 1931, with the adoption of the Hoover moratorium, all German payment or delivery of reparations ceased, and, although far from negligible, the extent of what Germany had paid and delivered up till then was nothing like what it had been intended to exact. This time, according to the confident prediction of President Roosevelt, early in 1945, there would be no disappointment over reparations; for they would be levied in kind. Roosevelt confined himself, when making his prediction, to speaking of the dismantling of German industry and of the removal of factories and plants to the territories of nations associated in the victory. We know now that at the conference of Yalta in February 1945, President Roosevelt, Mr. Churchill, and Marshal Stalin agreed also that German prisoners of war should be retained in the custody of at least most of the principal victors and their labour treated as part of reparations. And of course all that was confirmed at the conference of Berlin in July 1945. From that date German factories were dismantled and removed, cattle was taken away, forests were 'exploited', and so on. Also, till the summer of 1948 German prisoners of war were retained in Britain; and in the Middle East, in France, and in Russia many were still not being repatriated then.

You might suppose that, inasmuch as the unconditional surrender put Germany entirely at the mercy of her victors, it would have been enough simply to levy reparations in those two ways without explanation, and likewise without explanation to take all the punitive measures

14

against the vanquished which the overwhelming victory made possible. In 1871, after the Franco-Prussian war, France had to pay an indemnity of five milliard gold francs. The indemnity was the ransom of defeat, and victory was deemed to furnish the other side with title enough for its exaction. In 1919 and 1945 that would not do. Then the western victors, and each time especially the United States, were not content to seize the spoils which victory had put in their grasp. They felt that they must produce another and additional title to them. The only difference between 1919 and 1945 in that respect was that in 1945 the title was to be made seemingly unassailable. In 1919 a few words had been inserted into a treaty. In 1945 there was to be all the paraphernalia of a great trial.

But the verdict returned at the Trial could only have provided an unassailable title if the holding of the Trial had been above all suspicion. If, instead, the ostensible legality of the Trial was really fraudulent, the result must be that, not one, but two evils were perpetrated. If it would have been wrong to seize the spoils of victory simply in virtue of having the superior strength needed to seize them, then to have sought to justify the seizure by means of a trial was doubly wrong. The seizure was wrong *ex hypothesi*, and so, if illegal, the Trial was.

At first sight the passenger who travels by train with a spurious ticket seems more moral and law-abiding than the passenger who tries to travel without any ticket, for the first does recognize the law of railway travel and the second openly ignores it. But the law is broken in both cases, and, in fact, the first passenger is indictable for two offences, for travelling without paying his fare and for forgery.

Supposing the expectations and hopes for the future of international justice, to which the Trial gave rise, were baseless and false, and the Trial, far from extending the dominion of law, was an abuse of legality, then better to have seized the spoils of victory without it. For then, not only would the Trial have afforded no warrant to the victors for inflicting retribution on the vanquished, but in addition justice would have been degraded. The Trial would then have marked a turning point in the innermost history of western man such as was reached once before in the middle ages with the setting up of the Inquisition, and again at the French Revolution when inquisitorial methods were discarded from the judicial procedure of the Continent. The western victors would then have to stand forth as a trio of monstrous Tartuffes.

It is because many profound and disturbing questions thus confront us as a result of the great Nuremberg Trial of the former German leaders that this Trial must be regarded as profoundly significant. The Trial had two pretexts. One was that it would contribute to the future respect of peace. The other was that it would assist to broaden and spread the rule of law. *A priori* both pretexts are open to being doubted. Hence there could be no greater mistake than to imagine that the last word was said when the prison gates closed on the men sentenced to penal servitude and the trap opened under the men sentenced to hang. The last word cannot be said till those doubts have been resolved, one way or the other, for us all.

THE TITLE OR WARRANT was in the tribunal's verdict. The tribunal pronounced all but three of the accused guilty. It is no objection to that verdict that their guilt had been pre-determined. Before the war had ended, on 20 March 1945, the archbishop of York stood in the House of Lords and demanded that the men, whom he in advance styled 'criminals', should receive punishment. He distinguished among the Germans three classes of guilty. First, the 'master criminals', as he termed them—'Hitler, Himmler, and his gang'—who should be executed, he said, not for their political, but for their criminal offences. Secondly, the large class of persons who had carried out their orders. Thirdly, the whole German people. Regarding the third class—the German people—he said that they as a whole could not be entirely distinguished from the Nazis. They had for year after year supported Hitler with enthusiasm. But punishment was already falling on them in the destruction of their homes and the invasion of their country. At the time before the war had ended when the archbishop spoke in this way, he no doubt faithfully reflected the sentiments of perhaps a majority of the peoples of the British Commonwealth, of the United States, and of France, at least as regards 'Hitler, Himmler, and his gang'. A majority of the people of the victorious countries had already taken German guilt for granted. As it turned out, if not Hitler and Himmler —who were dead—at least 'his gang' were accused and sentenced for what the archbishop referred to as 'criminal offences' as well as for what he called 'political offences'. But certainly the guilt of 'his gang' had been pre-determined. If, however, the evidence heard at the Trial only served to confirm the popular sentiment of German guilt, the pre-determination of that guilt could not render the tribunal's verdict suspect.

But the title which the verdict of the tribunal gave to the victors for their after-war policy towards the vanquished was not only pre-determined; it was also self-conferred. And that constitutes an objection to the title which is not so easily disposed of. It was the vanquished who were tried and sentenced. It was the victors who decided on holding the Trial, appointed the judges,

17

and bestowed on them the 'law' which they were to administer. In effect, the victors judged and condemned the vanquished.

If it was wished to have the verdict unassailable, that did not do. In the first place, victors in a war never can be accepted as impartial judges.

In the second place, it could not follow automatically that the victors were entirely free of that same guilt of which the vanquished were convicted. Yet the victors could not sit in judgement on themselves, at least regarding the major charge of 'crimes against peace', nor could they invite the vanquished to judge them at the same time as they judged the vanquished. The alleged 'war guilt' of the vanquished, which it was professed to establish by means of the verdict of the tribunal, lay in their having gone to war. The major accusation at the Trial was that of responsibility for 'crimes against peace'. The former German leaders, that is to say, were pronounced guilty of 'planning and waging aggressive war or war in violation of international treaties'. The tribunal in its Judgement pronounced the accused to have been guilty of responsibility, in the course of waging their main so-called 'aggressive war', for incidental acts of aggression against countries at peace. But the judges were only the creatures of the victorious powers. If the governments of the victorious powers had also been guilty of acts of aggression against countries at peace, that surely constituted a serious disqualification of the tribunal. For the tribunal would then have been pronouncing penalties for acts said to have been committed by the vanquished and have been leaving similar acts committed by the victors unreproved. Certainly in that event there could be no question of the tribunal's verdict leading to an extension of the dominion of justice.

On two accounts, then, a serious objection to the validity of the title which the victors obtained from the

18

verdict of the tribunal is that this title was self-conferred.

On top of that, for the verdict of the tribunal to have constituted a valid title the main charge for which the former German leaders were put on trial—the charge in Count Two of the Indictment of responsibility for 'crimes against peace'—would have had to be established indubitably. But in truth this charge was one impossible to substantiate.

The statement may at first be astounding. There is no doubt that the German government declared war on certain countries and that its armies invaded other countries with which it was then at peace. The German government in 1939 declared war on Poland, in 1940 invaded Denmark and Norway, Holland, Belgium, and Luxembourg, in 1941 invaded Yugoslavia and Greece, and, in 1941 also, declared war on Russia and on the United States. In view of that chronology of wars declared and of invasions, it might seem that the accusation of responsibility for 'crimes against peace' rested on indisputable facts. But the so-called 'crimes against peace' alleged in the Indictment were not simply declarations of war against other countries and not even invasions of other countries without a declaration of war. The whole of the proceedings at Nuremberg was governed by the Charter which the victors jointly promulgated on 8 August 1945. In the Charter 'crimes against peace' was a term said to mean 'planning, preparation, initiation or waging of a war of aggression, or a war in violation of international treaties, agreements or assurances'. That is to say, it was neither declaration of war nor invasion without declaration, but 'wars of aggression' and 'wars in violation of treaties' with which the accused at Nuremberg were charged and of which twelve of them were held by the tribunal to be guilty. In speaking of a charge that could not possibly be substantiated, that is the charge I mean.

To see that it could not be substantiated is of fundamental importance for an understanding of the Trial. The charge was that the 'defendants', as they were styled, had, 'with divers other persons, participated in the planning, preparation, initiation and waging of wars of aggression, which were also wars in violation of international treaties, agreements, and assurances'. It would at least seem that the victorious powers who were sitting in judgement on the so-called 'defendants' were open to have an equivalent charge preferred against them.

On 30 November 1939 Russia declared war on and invaded Finland. Whatever the reasons for the conflict, so clearly did this war, 'initiated' by Russia, seem to be a war of aggression that on account of it Russia was expelled from the League of Nations. In the first quarter of 1940, Britain and France wanted to move troops through the neutral territory of Sweden. The intention was to reinforce the Finnish armies that were fighting against Russia, even though it was not proposed, I believe, that the two countries, Britain and France, should declare war on Russia. Russia was apparently to be attacked while at peace with them. The plan was abandoned because Sweden refused to give passage to the troops, and instead Russia, in the following year, became Britain's ally. On 8 April 1940 an expedition was to have left Britain in order to undertake a descent on Narvik in the neutral country of Norway. On 13 March, however, the Finnish government requested from the Russians an armistice, and the expedition was abandoned. In June 1940 Russia invaded the Baltic States of Estonia, Latvia, and Lithuania, with which countries Russia was at peace, and on 3 August of the same year those states were incorporated with the Russian Union. Early in 1941 Britain invaded and garrisoned Iceland. Although under the same king as Denmark, Iceland had been since 1918 a free and independent state. The German invasion of Denmark in 1940 had not made it belligerent territory. In July 1941, while ostensibly at peace with the world, the United States began sending troops to Iceland in order to relieve the British garrison. Later in 1941 Britain invaded and garrisoned the Azores, the Canaries, and the Cape Verde Islands, all of them at the time neutral territories. In November 1942 Britain and the United States invaded and garrisoned Algeria and French Morocco. The British and American technique for the invasion and occupation of neutral territories usually differed from the German. The neutral government concerned was first directed to ask for the protection which an invading force was supposed to provide. But in North Africa this preliminary, for good reasons, had to be dispensed with.

Algeria is an integral part of France, and, as regards the violation of international treaties, there was in force at the time an armistice signed with Germany in 1940 by the legal French government of the day. That armistice provided that Algeria would not have a German garrison, and in fact, when the British and American contingents landed, no German forces were there for them to attack. French Morocco had likewise no German garrison.

In the following year Britain without leave invaded and took temporary possession of the French island of Madagascar. In 1945 Russia declared war on Japan. Russian armies invaded Manchuria and Korea. Manchuria is a part of China, which the Japanese had transformed into the state of Manchukuo, and Korea had been independent. That both territories were in tutelage to Japan could be no argument for a failure to restore the *status quo ante*. Yet, after the Japanese surrender, the Russian government, while reaffirming respect of Chinese sovereignty over Manchuria, established military bases there. Korea was divided into two areas of rival occupation, one American, the other Russian, and in May 1946 the North of Korea became a Communist republic and a Russian satellite state.

To pretend that in all these invasions, occupations, annexations, and subjections, there had been no apparent 'aggression' and no 'violation of international treaties, agreements or assurances', would be more than otiose: it would be impudent. As regards Norway, for instance, the question was simply whether Britain or Germany should get there first. Hence, as I say, it might seem that if the former German leaders were open to being accused and convicted of the charge in Count Two of the Indictment—the charge of 'crimes against peace' —so were the members of the governments of Russia, Britain, and the United States, so (at least as regards intent) were the members of the French government that wanted to attack Russia in Finland in 1940, and so were the Frenchmen who set themselves up as a government in Algeria and, in 1944, assumed the government of France itself, for they recruited French troops to join in the war against Germany.

On top of all that, the accusation and conviction of former German leaders at Nuremberg of responsibility for 'crimes against peace' had a feature so bewildering as to appear incredible. The responsibility of which the former German leaders were accused and convicted included that for the invasion of Poland in September 1939. On this point the words of the international military tribunal, in its Judgement, were as follows: 'The tribunal is fully satisfied by the evidence that the war initiated by Germany against Poland on the 1st of September 1939 was most plainly an aggressive war.' Yet on 17 September 1939 Russia too invaded and promptly occupied half of Poland. That is to say, the Russian government had apparently done exactly what the German government had done. But while members

22

of that former German government were in the dock, and were convicted, the Russian government was represented among the prosecutors and the Russian government was represented on the bench. We there had something which, according to Dr. M. J. Bonn,[1]

has affronted the conscience of all those to whom justice is not a mere formal observation of rules of procedure, especially when those rules have been drafted for a particular purpose.

Regarding an affront to the conscience of people who still care for justice, Dr. Bonn may have been right, and yet up to the time at which he wrote the conscience of such people had proved singularly inarticulate.[2] But at any rate you will agree that if an ordinary decent man from the moon had landed at Nuremberg in 1946 and had been offered the spectacle of the Trial, he would have concluded that irrationality was master. Two parties had committed an act alleged to be a crime, and on the charge of having therefore been criminal one of the two parties was being tried by the other.

Nevertheless, in respect of the propriety of the accusation of responsibility for 'crimes against peace' when brought at Nuremberg by the victors against the van-

[1] 'The Crime of War and the Soviets' in *Contemporary Review*, No. 988, April 1948.
[2] Cf., however, an article entitled 'Ça y est' by Pasteur Jacques Ellul in *Réforme* (Paris), 12 October 1946; and also Major-General J. F. C. Fuller, *Armament and History* (1946), especially p. 176; Senator Robert A. Taft, 'Equal Justice Under Law', an address at Kenyon College, Gambier, Ohio, 5 October 1946; H. A. Smith, *The Crisis in the Law of Nations* (1947), pp. 46-8; Brigadier-General J. H. Morgan, K.C., *The Great Assize* (1948); speech by the duke of Bedford, Hansard, House of Lords, 16 October 1945; speech by the bishop of Chichester, Hansard, House of Lords, 23 June 1948. Other utterances have doubtless escaped me. Much of course was suppressed. But on the whole it is safe to say that both in Britain and the United States, as well as in France, the voices with legal authority and the chief voices of the church kept silent.

quished, appearances were deceptive. Nothing that the victors might have done with the semblance of 'aggression' or of 'violation of treaties' was relevant. For although the Charter and the Indictment specified 'aggression', and although it was 'invasion and aggression' that the tribunal, being bound by the Charter, held the evidence to have proved against twelve of the accused, neither 'aggression' nor 'violation of treaties' was the charge pressed by the prosecution. That is not surprising.

In the past nothing has been so easy as to be mistaken about 'aggression' even where aggression seems to have been most evident. A striking instance is supplied by Napoleon's invasion of Russia in 1812. Thiers, who, in being a member of several French governments, had practical experience of statecraft, and who also ranks as a great historian, was fifteen when the invasion took place. In writing of it, he was writing of something that had occurred within his own memory. In his *History of the Consulate and the Empire*—the last volume of which appeared in 1862—he laid it down that in going to war with Russia half a century earlier, in 1812, Napoleon was unquestionably the aggressor. His view came to be universally accepted by subsequent historians. But in our own day Mr. Louis Madelin has become the historian of Napoleon and his times, and in the volume entitled *La Crise de l'Empire*,[1] he advances and strongly supports the view that on this occasion there was no aggression by Napoleon. So with the immediate origins of other wars. A scholar strives to make his judgement emerge from a careful collection, collation, and weighing of evidence, only for some other scholar, after he is dead, to arise and refute him.

To decide about aggression, not, as Thiers sought to decide, fifty years after the event, but within a lustrum,

[1]*Paris*, 1945.

24

must of course be far more difficult. We now know a great deal more about the immediate origins of the war between the United States and Japan than the American people knew on the morrow of the Japanese attack on Pearl Harbor in December 1941. Indeed, we now know more than was made public at the trial in Tokio of Japanese so-called 'major war criminals', which opened on 3 May 1947 and ended in August 1948. We know it to have been contended that the late Franklin Roosevelt wished to bring the United States into the European war against Germany and in support of Britain. In 1941 a majority of the American people was of course opposed to intervention, and this was an obstacle to the fulfillment of Roosevelt's alleged plans and one which he is said to have set himself to overcome. It has been contended that he manoeuvred to provoke a Japanese attack. Not only had Japan ten years earlier invaded Manchuria and transformed that Chinese province into a Japanese satellite state; not only had Japan since 1937 been at war with China; but also Japan had recently invaded and occupied Indo-China. In July 1941 Roosevelt countered this latter occupation by having Japanese credits in the United States blocked. In spite, or as a result, of his action, the opportunity thereupon arose of settling amicably the differences between the two countries. In August a newly appointed Japanese foreign secretary, Admiral Toyada, had a long conversation with the United States ambassador in Tokio, Mr. Joseph C. Grew. Mr. Grew reported to Washington that the American show of firmness had been successful. The Japanese wanted to talk turkey. A conference might be arranged, and Prince Konoye, then Japanese prime minister, was ready to have it held on American soil. Mr. Grew explained that, as the prince's prestige would be involved, he would be certain to do everything possible for the sake of reaching an agreement. He added

25

that if the Japanese proposal for a conference were rejected, war appeared to be inevitable. Roosevelt did not accept the offer of an interview with the Japanese prime minister on American soil. Instead, he sent to Mr. Grew on 17 August a memorandum requiring that Japan should take no further steps to pursue 'the military domination of neighbouring countries'. As Prince Konoye could not produce an agreement with the United States, he fell from office. In October he was succeeded by General Tojo. The Japanese war party had taken the helm. On 26 November Roosevelt sent to the Japanese government what was virtually an ultimatum. Japan was to evacuate both China and Indo-China and Japan was to support no other Chinese government than the national government of China. The terms were of course unacceptable as they stood, and it was then that the Japanese government, under a threat of war from the United States, struck the first blow. A surge of indignation swept through the United States. Roosevelt, in order to ensure his country's intervention in Europe, needed to do no more. Germany of her own accord declared war on the United States.[1] That is one version. There are others. If we consider only Japan, we find that as early as September 1940, an influential section of leaders—the Japanese war party—had begun fostering a policy of territorial expansion southward and westward and was willing to risk war for the sake of its success. Moreover, the German government, as if bent on the destruction of Germany, had steadily pressed Japan to go to war. If, then, there was aggression in the war be-

[1]For the full account, cf. Forrest Davis and Ernest K. Lindley, *How War Came* (1942); Joseph C. Grew, *Ten Years in Japan* (1944); Elliott Roosevelt, *As He Saw It* (1946); Sumner Welles, *The Time for Decision* (1944) and *Where Are We Heading?* (1946); Henry L. Stimson, *Diary; The Memoirs of Cordell Hull* (1948); and, above all, Charles A. Beard, *President Roosevelt and the Coming of War 1941* (1948).

tween Japan and the United States, which side was the aggressor? Obviously, to return a true answer is not easy.

What does one historian overlook or remain unaware of that enables another historian to reverse his verdict? It must be certain factors in an invariably intricate complex of circumstances. To a German in 1939 who foresaw that the choice open to Poland was not between independence and dependence on Germany but between dependence on Germany and dependence on Russia, it could seem as iniquitous that Britain and France should go to war in support of Polish intransigence as to a Briton that Germany should decide to obliterate Poland once a settlement between Germany and the Polish government had become impossible. That is to say, international conflicts arise in reality, not owing to nefarious plans for 'aggression' on one side only, but because the resort to force is justified by either side on different grounds, and that those grounds of justification are in all likelihood mutually incomprehensible and certainly irreconcilable.

A party held to be the offender finds it easier to imagine others in its place than the parties passing judgment find it to imagine themselves in that of an alleged offender. Thrice the League of Nations strove to declare an instance of aggression—in 1931 as regards Japan and Manchuria; in 1935 as regards Italy and Abyssinia; in 1939 as regards Russia and Finland. All three efforts failed, because (exiles apart) no Japanese, no Italian, and no Russian could suppose for a moment that in like circumstances any great power represented in the League of Nations would have failed to act as Japan or Italy or Russia acted.

For the word 'aggression' to be applied with meaning in any particular instance, except as a technical term to designate, without pejorative significance, an actual declaration of war or a first act of hostilities, the party accused of 'aggression' would have to recognize *voluntarily*

27

that an aggression had in fact been committed. This recognition it has of course proved quite impossible to obtain; for no national government is ever conscious of being an 'aggressor'. In all sincerity its conscience is invariably clear. When the allegation of 'aggression' is put forward, not by a group of onlookers—who, if not understanding, could at least pretend to be disinterested—but by one party against the other party to a war, the word necessarily loses all credit. For it is too obviously in the interest of one side in a war to put the whole blame on the other side.

That is why, as regards the accusation and conviction of former German leaders at Nuremberg of 'crimes against peace', whatever the victors may have done during the war in the way of man-handling peace is irrelevant. War is expensive and extremely hasardous, and no country goes to war without an object. The object may be the protection of what are thought to be 'special and vital interests', and therefore technical 'self-defence', or else it may be to fulfill what is interpreted as a treaty obligation. In any event, the nature of the object is not a matter of fact: it is a matter of opinion.

Even at Nuremberg these elementary truths were exemplified. The accused were allowed counsel to defend them. These counsel submitted that the question when and why a sovereign state should go to war was a question to be decided by that state alone. A state could not be denied the power to decide that question without being denied at the same time its very sovereignty. It was, presumably, because this plea had been advanced that the prosecution did not press the naked charge of 'aggression' contained in Count Two. Instead, the prosecution appeared to accept the plea, at least to the extent of seeking to confute it.

The argument employed in confutation was illuminating. It betrayed plainly how impossible it was for the prosecution to substantiate the charge in Count Two. The argument may be summed up in some words used by the chief prosecutor in behalf of the British government, Sir Hartley Shawcross, then attorney-general. In the course of his speech closing the British government's case against the so-called 'major war criminals', he allowed himself the following pronouncement:[1]

The Pact of Paris did not take away the right of self-defence. Admittedly every sovereign state is the judge whether action in self-defence is necessary. But that does not mean that the state thus acting is the ultimate judge of the propriety and of the legality of its conduct. It acts at its peril.

The intent at least of this passage was unmistakable. The speaker could not have been reproached with obscurity. But surely it was very naïve of the chief British prosecutor to have argued after this fashion. For what does the argument amount to? A sovereign state is at liberty to go to war in defence of what it thinks its interests, and when it does thus go to war, it is the sole judge of what constitutes 'self-defence'. But if that sovereign state is then defeated, its judgement ceases to be valid, and it is the victors who are called upon to decide whether or not the resort to war ostensibly in 'self-defence' had 'propriety' and 'legality'. It was no longer 'aggression' of which the former German leaders were being accused; it was mis-judging the nature of 'self-defence'. That was, I need hardly say, entirely novel doctrine. It was also an argument highly vulnerable. According to Sir Hartley Shaw-cross, in the speech from which I have quoted the above passage, the British government attached 'great impor-tance' to 'the firm establishment of the legal aspect of the crime against peace'. The British government could not have gone about establishing its so-called 'legal aspect'

[1] *The Times* (London), 27 July 1946.

more lamely. Indeed, there could have been no better way of establishing that what was termed 'the crime against peace' cannot be a crime in law.

Sir Hartley Shawcross dealt with the case of a state that went to war ostensibly in 'self-defence' and then was defeated. What of the state that went to war on the same pretext and then was victorious? Who could decide on the 'propriety' and 'legality' of the conduct of this latter state? Sir Hartley did not say. His silence is understandable. He could not have said without exposing the fallaciousness of his reasoning. On his argument, had Germany won the war, the German government might equally well have argued that the victorious powers, which then would have been the vanquished, could not be 'the ultimate judges' of the 'propriety' and 'legality' of their having resorted to war, and that the judge of their conduct was now the German government. Indeed, there is nothing to prevent Germans from arising in a proximate future—and it is only too probable that they will arise—to argue that, even though defeated in 1945, Germany went to war in 1939 in protection of 'special and vital interests' and hence in technical 'self-defence', and in December 1941 went to war in fulfillment of a treaty obligation. What would there be to gainsay them? Simply the Judgement rendered by the international military tribunal at Nuremberg. And that Judgement is worthless.

It is worthless, in the first place, because the tribunal was but the creature and instrument of the victors. No doubt the prosecution, and the governments which the prosecution represented, would have liked the tribunal to be accepted, since it was styled 'international', as not exclusively composed of delegates and servants of the victorious powers. No doubt the prosecution would have liked the tribunal to be accepted as having embodied the conscience of civilized mankind. But this conscience had not appointed it. It was not 'international' in that sense.

Admittedly, seventeen countries, or it may have been nineteen, had approved of the prosecution of Germans as 'war criminals'. They could not confer on the tribunal any super-national jurisdiction. For it was not constituted by super-national authority. There was and is no such authority. It follows that the international military tribunal was 'international' only in the sense that, for example, the bridge which links the French frontier town of Hendaye with the Spanish frontier town of Irún is an international bridge. The tribunal was international only in the sense that more than one nation was represented on it. Actually, as we know, it represented no more than four nations. And those four nations happened to be the four chief victorious powers. Consequently, the tribunal was the judiciary of prejudiced parties. The tribunal was merely the prolongation of the prosecution. It was the prosecution on the bench in addition to the prosecution at the prosecutors' stand. Its Judgement was unacceptable. Its Judgement was as unacceptable regarding the validity of 'self-defence' in a particular instance as it was unacceptable regarding the occurrence of 'aggression'. For victors in a war never can be accepted as impartial judges.

The Judgement was worthless, in the second place, because if it was possible for the vanquished to be mistaken regarding their need of going to war in 'self-defence', it was equally possible for the victors. Nothing could confer on the victors a power of judgement superior to that of the vanquished. The latter were no more and no less prone to be fallible than the former. For, exactly like 'aggression', the existence of a need to defend 'special and vital interests' by resort to war is not a matter of fact: it is a matter of opinion.

Of course other factors besides the supposed need of defending 'special and vital interests' weigh with the government of a sovereign state when it is deciding if that state shall go to war. For one thing, there has to be the confidence of victory, or, in the event of invasion, the sentiment that independence must be defended, even hopelessly. But confidence of victory cannot be grounded in fact. There may be crushing superiority, but nobody can foresee the future. Confidence of victory must be based on opinion. Opinion likewise is the basis of the sentiment that independence must be defended in any circumstances. Holland resisted the German invaders in 1939 for four days and lost a quarter of its army. Denmark did not resist at all. Who shall say that Denmark suffered more than Holland in the sequel?

You may tell me that, whatever the force of the objections there were to preferring against the former German leaders a charge of responsibility for 'aggression', at least it is indisputable that Germany went to war, not once, but repeatedly, 'in violation of international treaties, agreements or assurances'. Certainly, the Indictment enumerated twenty-six treaties or agreements which the German government was alleged to have violated. However that may have been, it is not worth looking into. For although the sanctity of treaties has been a convenient shibboleth whereby war-time propaganda identifies the corrupt nature of an enemy, the respect or repudiation of an international treaty at any particular time has always depended on circumstances, and the interpretation of the circumstances is one more matter of opinion. It is simply not true that a state has the obligation to respect an international treaty to which it has subscribed if subsequent events lead the government of that state to believe that the provisions of the treaty have become inapplicable. Here on the subject are the words of a former Lord Chancellor:[1]

Technical considerations have in practice no great weight in a discussion as to the effect of treaties between states, impor-

[1] Lord Maugham, *The Truth about the Munich Crisis* (1944), pp. 74-5.

32

tant as they might be in contracts between private persons; for there is a weighty implication to be borne in mind in construing treaties between nations, namely, that according to good sense and to the practice of civilized nations the obligations they contain are regarded as subject to the implied condition that the circumstances under which they were made have not materially changed. In other words, the condition *rebus sic stantibus* is held to apply. It has been held to apply by Gladstone, Theodore Roosevelt, Woodrow Wilson, Sir Edward Grey, and others. Cf. *The Twenty Years' Crisis* by E. H. Carr, chapter 'The Sanctity of Treaties'.

If the passage correctly summarizes accepted practice—and I imagine that no defender of the preposterous thesis that resort to war was already in 1939 'an international crime' would deny, on being confronted with the passage, that it does correctly summarize accepted practice—the opinion of one state that 'conditions have' 'materially changed' is as good as the opinion of another, and no state, or coalition of states, has any support from international law for accusing another state or the former leaders of that state of 'crime', when that other state has seen fit to repudiate an international treaty.

I have now shown you that it is only too easy to be mistaken about the occurrence of 'aggression', and that hitherto a definition of the term 'aggression' which would be acceptable to both sides in a conflict has proved quite impossible to arrive at. I have shown you that the British prosecution at Nuremberg was prepared to admit that the former German leaders in the dock may have thought, when they declared war in behalf of their country, that the war was in 'self-defence', and that the British prosecution followed the admission of this by asserting that in that event the former German leaders had misjudged; and yet that, although the accusation of having misjudged a need of 'self-defence' is one that any victor might bring against any vanquished, it is not an accusation that can be proved. I have shown you that it has been commonly accepted hitherto that observance of an international treaty by any one of its signatories must depend on the opinion of that signatory that the conditions in which the treaty was concluded have not materially changed. It is for all those reasons that we are bound to conclude that the charge in Count Two of the Indictment at Nuremberg—the charge of 'crimes against peace'—could not possibly be substantiated. The victors arraigned the vanquished in the dock after the war of 1939–45 on an illusory charge.

A CHARGE 'of the utmost gravity'. So the international military tribunal at Nuremberg in its Judgement characterized the charge of responsibility for 'crimes against peace'. The tribunal also declared that 'a war of aggression is the supreme international crime, differing only from other war crimes in that it contains within itself the accumulated evil of the whole'. And it is of course true that the charges contained in two other counts of the Indictment, Count Two—which contained the charge of responsibility for so-called 'war crimes'—and Count Three —which contained the charge of responsibility for so-called 'crimes against humanity'—were subordinate to the charge contained in Count Two of responsibility for 'crimes against peace'. For unless there had been war there could have been no 'war crimes', and, so long as war had not befallen and had not been won, the so-called 'crimes against humanity' which were said to have taken place inside Germany failed to arouse the judicial instincts of the victors any more than other similar deeds elsewhere were, as we shall see, to rouse those instincts

34

afterwards. Hence I at first supposed that the charge of responsibility for 'crimes against peace', which I have been considering, was the most serious and the most important of the charges preferred against the former German leaders at the Trial. But I have since changed my mind. No doubt from the moment the war began allied propaganda—that directed to neutrals as well as that intended to keep the popular fighting spirit ebullient—laid heavy emphasis on its allegation that Germany was responsible if differences had not been settled peaceably. But it now seems to me that by the time the war was over and won, that allegation of 'crimes against peace' might have roused little indignation in the victorious peoples, but for the supplementary allegations of 'war crimes' and of 'crimes against humanity'. And then the prosecution and punishment of the so-called 'major war criminals' might have been palsied from want of the firm support of popular clamour. It was from the allegation that Germans had committed the most appalling 'war crimes' on a colossal scale and the most horrible 'crimes against humanity' that the alleged 'crimes against peace' derived their full enormity. The accusations contained in Counts Three and Four of the Indictment made the 'crime' alleged in Count Two more grim and lurid. The illusory 'crime' of 'aggressive war' was the more heinous in that, in being held to have committed it, the men in the dock at Nuremberg could be alleged responsible for the deaths 'of ten million combatants killed in battle', and, 'at the lowest computation', for

Twelve million men, women, and children, done to death, not in battle or in passion, but in the cold, calculated attempt to destroy nations and races.

I quote the words uttered at the Trial by the chief prosecutor in behalf of the British government.

Furthermore, it was on the ground that Germans in great number had committed 'war crimes' and 'crimes against humanity' that the prosecution and punishment of so-called 'war criminals' at the hands of the seventeen countries represented in the war crimes commission became such a vast and prolonged undertaking.

Hence the charges contained in Counts Three and Four of the Indictment may have been even more important in effect than the charge on which they no doubt depended—the charge of responsibility for 'crimes against peace'.

Working through various subcommittees, the war crimes commission drew up and published eighty lists containing altogether the names of about forty thousand persons to be 'charged as war criminals', the majority of these persons being Germans. Before the war had come to an end, offices were opened and investigating teams were constituted in enemy territory. Incidentally, Russia was not represented on the war crimes commission, and the trial before the international military tribunal at Nuremberg formed the only proceedings in which Russia was associated with the western victors. That does not mean, however, that the Russian government did not hold other trials too.

Shortly after the German surrender the trials of persons on the lists of the war crimes commission began. The first of such trials was, I believe, that of the persons in charge of the German concentration camp at Belsen in the area in British occupation. It was held at Lüneburg. By the end of 1946, about 24,400 persons had been tried on the Continent of Europe in British, American, French, Greek, Norwegian, Czecho-Slovak, and Polish courts specially set up for the purpose. Of these 24,400 persons, 1,432 were sentenced to death, 16,400 were sent to prison for varying terms, and about 6,500 were acquitted. In the Far East 1,470 persons were tried, 457 of them being sentenced to death and 735 to prison. In the area of Germany in British occupation the courts were formed in virtue of a warrant specially issued to the army by the Crown in the summer of 1945. In the American zone the procedure was laid down by ordinance, and a similar instrument was provided for the French zone.

There were yet other trials. The international military tribunal at Nuremberg had to adminster some kind of 'law', and the 'law' was delivered to it by means of a Charter which the four principal victorious powers promulgated on 8 August 1945. In this Charter the tribunal was directed to decide if the term 'criminal organization' was applicable to the former German government, to each of various groups and associations of the dissolved German National Socialist party, and also to the German high command. The tribunal, in its Judgement, delivered on 30 September and 1 October 1946, did declare four of these associations to be 'criminal'. They were: (1) the *Schutzstaffeln* or S.S., originally a branch of the private army of the National Socialist party, but subsequently developed into two groups, one police, the other military; (2) the *Korps der politischen Leiter*, or leadership corps of the party; (3) the *Sicherheitsdienst*, or security police; and (4) the *Gestapo*, or secret state police.

The Control Council appointed by the four powers was the legislative as well as the administrative body in Germany after the surrender. Under Law No. 10, promulgated by this council on 20 December 1945, it became a crime to have been a member of any 'group or organization declared criminal by the international military tribunal'. In the expectation of the tribunal's Judgement, about 45,000 civilians had been taken into custody in North-West Germany alone—the area in British occupation—and they were kept in custody for more than a year without trial. In this same area, 19,500 of these internees were selected for trial, and before nearly a hundred courts their trials began in June 1947. The courts were set up in the same way as the courts that tried persons accused of 'war crimes'. To all intents and purposes they were the same courts. In order to realize the size of the total number of so-called 'criminals' involved, it has to be remembered that courts were busy on a like scale in both the French and American zones.

Yet further, in Article 6 of the Charter, 'the planning, preparation and waging of aggressive war' was defined as a 'crime', and 'organizers' and 'accomplices' were declared to be among those 'responsible for all acts performed by any persons in execution of such plan'. On this Charter authority, and in virtue also of Control Council Law No. 10, already mentioned, the United States government instituted at Nuremberg in 1947 courts for the trial of persons accused of having been outstanding 'organizers' or 'accomplices'. In contradistinction to the international military tribunal, these courts were purely American. Among persons brought before them were Field-Marshal Ehrardt Milch, of the German air force; German doctors and heads of medical services; generals, colonels, and others of the S.S.; fifteen jurists; twenty-four directors and officials of the I. G. Farbenindustrie; and twelve directors and officials of Krupps. Three field-marshals, nine generals of the army, and one admiral were tried together. Still other American trials took place at Dachau.

Regarding the conduct of these wholesale trials, the public of the victorious nations knew little. That Field-Marshal Milch appealed to Washington against his sentence was, for instance, never disclosed in England. Details of the controversy behind the scenes that led to the adjournment of the I. G. Farbenindustrie trial immediately after it had opened and delayed a resumption till many months later, were not communicated to the public of the West. Yet in all the other trials, in addition to the first Nuremberg Trial, whether trials of so-called 'war criminals', trials of members of the allegedly 'criminal organizations', or trials of 'organizers' and 'accomplices', the same issues were at stake as in the great Trial itself. At Nuremberg the so-called 'major war criminals' were accused, and all but three were found guilty, not only of alleged direct offences of their own, but also of ultimate responsibility for all the offences said to have been committed by Germans termed 'war criminals' without qualification or by alleged 'organizers' or 'accomplices'. The accusations brought against the former German leaders at Nuremberg thus typified all the accusations that were the pretext of the multitude of other trials. For that reason, if the qualification of the western victors to sit in judgement on individuals among the vanquished needs to be scrutinized, it will be enough to consider the Nuremberg Trial.

Those western victors instituted the Nuremberg Trial in order, as I have suggested, to confer on themselves a title to mete out retribution and to levy reparations. But they really required a title also in order to institute that Trial and all the other trials. Was there one? They were, they said, the aggrieved party, and an aggrieved party may institute a prosecution. They were drawing a false analogy. When a sovereign state prosecutes one of its citizens or a foreigner who is bound to respect its laws because within its gates, that state stands as the representative of human society. It is human society that is understood to depend for its existence and prosperity on the maintenance of law and order, and human society that therefore punishes the breach of law and order. A sovereign state is able to stand for human society in those circumstances because it is law and order that the state is anxious to safeguard and not a special category of persons that it is anxious to punish. The analogy which the western victors sought to draw in describing themselves as the aggrieved party was an analogy between a sovereign state that stands for human society and themselves jointly prosecuting and punishing individuals among the vanquished on the score that these had been guilty of breaches of international law and order. And the analogy was false because, as regards 'war crimes' and so-called 'crimes against humanity', the victors were solely concerned to prosecute and to punish a special category of persons.

In October 1945 the Control Council for Germany issued a proclamation to the German people. The proclamation made known judicial reforms and a new judicial system. Its first clause contained the following affirmation: 'All persons are equal before the law.'[1] The principle thus reaffirmed is one common to modern jurisprudence, and it is obviously fundamental to any discharge of justice. Whether or not a given criminal law, a given penal code, or even a particular court, is faithful to the principle, and all persons without distinction are amenable to its jurisdiction, will afford a clear test for any claim that the preservation of law and order is the object.

In order to put the trials to that test, it is only necessary to ask who were the so-called 'war criminals', the members of so-called 'criminal organizations', the alleged 'organizers' and 'accomplices'? In February 1946 the English under-secretary for war treated the House of Commons to a definition of the term 'war criminal'. He then made it plain that a 'war criminal' so called could not be merely a person who had, or who might have, committed a 'war crime' or a 'crime against humanity'. He had also to be a German (or national of some Axis state). He had to be one of the vanquished. The citizen of an allied state who might be prosecuted by the authorities of that state on account of his activities during the war could not be,

[1] *The Times* (London), 23 October 1945.

the under-secretary said,[1] a 'war criminal'; such a citizen was a 'quisling'. For that matter, the only offences connected with the war of which even a so-called 'quisling' could be guilty, or could be accused, were, apparently, offences held to have been to the detriment of the powers and of the armed forces which in the end secured victory. No citizen or soldier of an allied state could be accused of a 'war crime' against Germans, nor of a 'crime against humanity'. It is thus clear that so-called 'war criminals' had to be either Germans or citizens of an Axis state. The Charter applied to Germany only, and, so far as trials of so-called 'war criminals' and other trials instituted by the western victors in Germany after the war are concerned, the accused were all Germans.

The implication was that no violations of the recognized rules of warfare, no so-called 'war crimes' of any kind, and no 'crimes against humanity', had been or were being committed by the victors and their armed forces. Was the implication true? Let us see. The kinds of 'war crimes' and the kinds of 'crimes against humanity' specified in the Indictment presented at Nuremberg were many. For the sake of simplicity, I shall refer only to the kinds of 'war crime' and the kinds of 'crime against humanity' which the international military tribunal named in its Judgement. The tribunal in that Judgement named six kinds of 'war crime' and two kinds of 'crime against humanity'. The kinds of "war crime" were: (1) Murder, ill-treatment, or deportation to slave labour of civilians of occupied territories; (2) Use of concentration camps to destroy opposition; (3) Murder or ill-treatment of prisoners of war; (4) Killing of hostages; (5) Plunder; and (6) Destruction of cities, towns, and villages, and devastation not justified by military necessity. The two kinds of 'crime against humanity' were the persecution,

[1]Hansard, 4 February 1946.

repression, and murder of political opponents in Germany and the persecution of Jews. Let me proceed on the basis of these two lists.

IN ANY VIEW of the conduct of the victors throughout the war with Germany one factor is easily overlooked. Yet it is only fair to take this factor into account. All possibility of committing 'war crimes' ceased for Germans with the surrender in May 1945 of the German armed forces. For the victors, on the contrary, that was largely when the possibility began. The victors could not deal well or ill with the inhabitants of occupied territory till territory had been invaded and occupied. Most if not all prisoners of war in German hands had been released by the end of hostilities. Those in the hands of the victors remained in captivity. Likewise, plunder and loot were not available to the victors till German property was all around them. If, then, there is to be comparison, it is the conduct of Germany's victors after the German surrender that needs to be compared with the conduct of the vanquished during the war.

However, that is speaking of the victors collectively. Among them was one exception. Almost as soon as the first German soldier invaded foreign territory, Russian armies too invaded and occupied foreign territory. The Russians had an early opportunity of committing so-called 'war crimes', and promptly the opportunity was taken. Listed in the Indictment of the so-called 'major war criminals' before the tribunal at Nuremberg as kinds of 'war crime' were mass deportations from 'occupied territories' of able-bodied citizens, in such conditions of transport that many died, and overcrowding them, allowing them insufficient clothing, leaving them for days with little or no food, the torture, beating, and hanging of them, the imprisonment of them without judicial process; letting civilians from 'occupied territory' die of starvation, debility, or 'supposedly natural causes'. Deeds of these kinds are on record as having been done by the Russian government, its soldiers, policemen, and officials, from the moment in September 1939 when, Russia and Poland being at peace, the eastern half of Poland became 'occupied territory'; became, that is to say, Polish territory in Russian military occupation. Deeds of these kinds are on record as having been done by the Russian government, and its minions, once the Baltic States—Estonia, Latvia, and Lithuania—were overrun by the Russian armies without declaration of war.

Of what happened in Poland a matter of fact account is contained in a book published in English during the summer of 1946. It is a book based on official material and documents of the exiled Polish government of the late General Sikorski. It is called *The Dark Side of the Moon*. To read it is harrowing, for it is largely made up of personal narratives and it abounds in detailed information. Its veracity has not been impugned. On the contrary, several English reviewers drew attention to its veracity. Notably, Mr. Edward Crankshaw stated that its general statements were confirmed by his own independent sources.[1] Its testimony is supported, moreover, by that of three earlier books in English and one in French. In English, Miss Odette Keun[2], Mr. Arthur Koestler,[3] and Mr. W. L. White,[4] had all dealt previously with the same happenings. The book in French is *La Justice soviétique* by Sylvestre Mora and Pierre Zwiernak.[5] *The*

[1] *The Spectator* (London), 13 July 1946.
[2] *Continental Stakes* (1944).   [3] *The Yogi and the Commissar* (1945).
[4] *Report on the Russians* (1945).   [5] Rome, 1945.

43

Dark Side of the Moon is simply the fullest account of the happenings that has appeared in any language. The information which it contains is of a kind seldom brought out of Russia. It became available only because, under the terms of the Russo-Polish treaty signed in London on 30 July 1941, and in virtue of the Russo-Polish military convention signed in Moscow in the following August, thousands of Poles who had been deported into Russia were released, and they narrated their experiences.

Mass deportations from Eastern Poland into Russia took place in February, April, and June 1940, and in June 1941. They occurred again after Russia, on 26 April 1943, broke off diplomatic relations with the Polish government in London, and all Polish citizens of the annexed area of Poland—said to be Ukrainians, Eastern Ruthenians, and Jews—were decreed by Russia to be Soviet citizens. There have been various estimates of the numbers deported. The recital of the figures sounds like a magnification of '*Madamina, il catalogo*', Leporello's song in the first act of *Don Giovanni*. Whereas, for some reason or other, the seduction of a whole regiment of women is funny, there was nothing funny about these deportations in droves and herds. It is beyond doubt that many thousands of men, women, and children were uprooted from their homes. The deported went to one of three destinations. These were: so-called 'free exile', prison, and lagier.

'Free exile' was the least horrible. But it was bad enough. Miss Ada Halpern has described what an experience it is.[1] It was her own. She was an actuary. She leads her readers to suppose that she had neither committed nor been accused of any criminal or political offence. Certainly she underwent no 'judicial process', such as the German so-called 'war criminals' were ac-

[1]*Liberation—Russian Style* (London, 1945); entitled in the United States *Conducted Tour*.

cused of having failed to provide. One morning, at about half-past two, she opened her door in reply to a ring, and found standing outside two officers of the N.K.V.D—the Russian police—and also some Russian soldiers. She, her sister, who was still a child, and her mother, who was ill, were told to pack at once. From the town in Poland in which they had their home, they were conveyed by rail in a crowded cattle truck to Kazakhstan. The journey lasted fourteen days. When they got out of the train she noticed that the party included two acquaintances of hers, a man of eighty-four and his wife aged eighty. Nobody could be too old for deportation, nobody too young. She and her sister were put to work on a *sovkhoz*, a Soviet agricultural management unit. The mother was allowed to remain with them. They had to make shift to find quarters and moved into an untenanted mud hut, where they had to share a room three yards by five with seven other persons. She had of course to improvise any cooking apparatus. She was put to work digging up frozen manure.

For the less fortunate among the deported there might be the second destination—prison. In Russia, according to *The Dark Side of the Moon*, prisons are not penal institutions. They are places in which suspected persons are detained 'pending inquiry'. Conditions in them can differ little if at all from the conditions in which the German concentration camps were found by the invading armies of the West. They are overcrowded. The semi-starvation, the filth, the neglected sick, the running sores, the rags, the despair, cannot be conveyed to any one who has always slept and breakfasted in comfort. Then there are the questionings, which invariably take place at night. They may be accompanied by beating and torture.

The third destination for deported Poles was lagier. A lagier is described as 'a corrective labour camp', to which persons are sent on being sentenced. Russia has an abundance of courts. There are supreme courts, people's courts, and five kinds of special court. Nevertheless, persons taken into custody for political reasons—and the deported Poles were all regarded as political offenders—commonly have their sentence signified on notice. There is no 'judicial process'. A sentence usually ranges from three to eight years. A sentence once completed may be renewed by means of a mere stroke of the pen. The living conditions in a lagier are extremely primitive. The diet is meagre. The convicts are clad in odds and ends of material. Murder for the sake of a garment is not unknown, and it is likely to go unpunished. Some lagiers are situated in areas where the climate allows only the most stalwart to survive.

Many Poles were deported direct to a lagier. A Polish artist, residing at present in England but having relatives still in Poland, and therefore unwilling to disclose his name, has stated, for instance, that he was arrested in Eastern Poland in June 1940. He, his wife, his mother-in-law, his pregnant sister-in-law and the latter's husband, with their daughter two years old, were taken to Ust Lobva, Oblast Svyerdlovsk, in the north-west of Siberia. They were put into a cattle truck with about fifty-five others in a train of forty trucks. The journey lasted forty-two days. Once every few days they were let out for a few moments. The rest of the time they were locked in. They had to make use of a hole in the floor of the truck. Every other day they were each given some boiled water and a small mug of *kasha* (a kind of porridge). The two-year old baby died during this journey. On arrival at their destination, the artist's brother-in-law was sent to work in a mine and died within a week. The widow, the artist's sister-in-law, gave birth to a baby weighing 2 lb. It died on the third day. The artist and his wife were put to work cutting timber in a forest. But they were not allowed to work together. The husband was in a party that went out each morning to one bank of the River Lala, the wife in a party that went to the other bank. They had to be afoot at four o'clock in order to begin work at seven, and, with a break in the middle of the day, work went on till late at night. They were told that they would each be paid five roubles a day, but in fact the payment, on the plea of necessary deductions, did not give them more than one rouble a day, and they were far from being able to get enough to eat. By the time they were released, in October 1941, they were in rags, they had both lost their teeth, and on their emaciated bodies were running sores and ulcers. They were directed to go to Buzuluk, a rallying-point for released Poles, but they were given no funds for the journey. Only thanks to the charity of poor Russians at the wayside did they get food during the five weeks that elapsed before they reached their destination.

Poland was not the only country to be invaded, while at peace with Russia, by the Russian armies. After the invasion of Eastern Poland, there was the invasion of the Baltic States. While the German armies were overrunning France in June 1940, Russian armies were marching into Estonia, Latvia, and Lithuania. Thereupon, from these countries also thousands of men and women considered to be unsympathetic in their politics were deported into the Russian hinterland. Then it was the turn of the German armies. They swept into the Baltic States, and behind them came the *Organisation Todt* with its inordinate demands for labour. But once the German armies had been driven back, and the three countries were again under Russian sway, the deportations into Russia were resumed. The whole lamentable story, especially as it concerns Estonia, has been told by Professor Ants Oras.[1] According to him—and he inspires

[1] *The Baltic Eclipse* (1948). Cf. also Bernard Newman, *Baltic Background* (1948).

47

credence—it has been Russian policy to disperse Estonians, Latvians, and Lithuanians all over the Soviet Union and to have their children brought up as Russians. Silence settled over the once animated town of Tartu (or Dorpat) as the systematic destruction of race and culture gathered impetus.

Almost simultaneously with the Russian invasion of the Baltic States in June 1940, Russia delivered an ultimatum to Rumania, and as a result obtained the cession of Bessarabia and North Bukovina. These territories were formed into a republic federated with the rest of the Russian Union, and from them too many of the inhabitants were deported into the interior of Russia, going either to 'free exile' or to corrective labour camps.

In view of all this, it was only to be expected that when the Russian armies at last penetrated into Germany in 1945, that kind of 'war crime' which the Charter, the Indictment, and the international military tribunal, in its Judgement, defined as the 'murder, ill-treatment, or deportation to slave labour or for any other purpose of the civilian population of occupied territory' would be committed wholesale. And this is what happened. A novel depicting the lot of the inhabitants of the Russian zone of Germany from shortly before the advent of the invaders down to the compulsory fusion of the Social Democrat party with the Communist party, renamed the Socialist Unity party, was published in Switzerland in 1947.[1] Anybody who has spent some time in Berlin with eyes and ears open knows that, although the story told in this novel is fiction, its detail is fact. To read it is an easy way of informing oneself of what otherwise is

[1]Karl Wilhelm, *Zwischen Braun und Rot* (Winterthur). An English translation entitled *Between Brown and Red* is being prepared for publication in the United States by Henry Regnery Company. The author has completed a second novel, dealing with life in Berlin. It is called *Brandenburger Tor*.

48

only to be learned from conversations and individual narratives. Many owners of factories were shot. One, for example, only owed his life to his workpeople, who pretended to the Russians that he was but the manager. Landowners were dispossessed, and left to fend for themselves as best they might. Women found in the street were undressed and raped in public. Small parties of Russian soldiers entered homes, and one after the other raped the housewife in the presence of her husband, who was forcibly held by those who either were waiting their turn or had had it. Not once, but repeatedly, homes were occupied by soldiery for weeks at a time, and they left behind them rooms denuded of furnishings, the bedsteads, for instance, having no more than the bare springs. Food became very scarce, and households who had anything to barter were impelled now and then to go to the black market, so that they might taste a morsel of meat and a little fat. To begin with, the black market was in the hands of Russian soldiers, who sought to drive extortionate bargains. For instance, in exchange for a ring worth $1,250, the most even a determined woman could obtain from a Russian private at his stall was 4 lb. meat, 4 lb. flour, and 2 lb. butter.

There were repeated drives to enlist German labour, skilled and unskilled, for work in Russia. They culminated in the operation named *Ossawakim*, which involved a comprehensive transfer of workers. The recruitment of labour for work in Russia was carried out partly by the Russians themselves in factories and camps directly in their control and partly through the agency of the German labour organization. No exact figures are obtainable, but among technicians and engineers the numbers appear to have been particularly high, and a figure of three thousand was repeatedly mentioned as being approximately correct. By various means ranging from open recruitment by contract to kidnapping, more than

200,000 workers and their families were deported to Russia.[1] In August 1946 it was noted that persons between the ages of fifteen and eighteen were arrested and taken to special camps for 'political re-education'.[2]

Altogether, there can be no doubt that civilians in the area of Germany in Russian occupation suffered 'ill-treatment or deportation', and that some were murdered. But in Germany the Russians were not alone. Germany was also invaded from the West. As the British, American, and French troops made their victorious advance, they behaved with all the licence and savagery of some primitive horde. Looting is forbidden by British military law on pain of heavy penalties. On this occasion the British command tacitly encouraged it among all ranks. Mr. Leonard O. Mosley, a war correspondent with the armies, found it, he says,[3] 'surprising how the looting fever attacked even the staidest members of the [British] Army'. There was an orgy of senseless destruction. Mr. Mosley says that a man in charge of a fishpond, on seeing a party of British soldiers approach, stood with his net ready to catch the fish for them. They preferred instead to throw hand grenades into the pond. The man could not understand it. 'There were the refugees too', Mr. Mosley also says.[4] The thousands of foreigners whom the German government had brought into Germany, to assist the war effort, and who, after the surrender, became known as 'displaced persons', were let loose to loot and to destroy while protected from Germans whom they despoiled.

Nor did the exploitation and spoliation of German civilians cease with the surrender. The 'Hague Rules' is the name given to the stipulations contained in the annex

[1]Peter Nettle, 'Inside the Russian Zone, 1945-1947' in *The Political Quarterly*, vol. XIX, No. 3, July-October 1948.

[2]*The Times* (London), 19 August 1946.

[3]*Report from Germany* (1945), p. 45.

[4]Ibid., p. 50.

to the convention concerning the laws and customs of war on land which was signed at The Hague in 1907. The convention was ratified by the governments of Britain and the United States as well as by those of many other countries. The Hague Rules governing the occupation of enemy territory are Nos. 42 to 56. Rule No. 52 was quoted by the international military tribunal, in its Judgement, and the tribunal declared that the rule had been broken by the Germans. But what of the British, the Americans, and the French? The rule states that 'private personal property not susceptible of direct military use must not be taken unless actually required for the needs of the army'. Yet British soldiers came home on leave from the Army of the Rhine weighed down with loot. There was a tremendous traffic in cigarettes, which became a second and better currency than the mark. When a Belgian woman visiting the British zone gave a German a cigarette in the presence of an official of the Control Commission, the latter rebuked her. 'Make him give you something for it', he said. 'You must not let him have it for nothing.' At these words the Belgian woman realized that German civilians were being made to give up their possessions in exchange for the cigarettes with which they could obtain food.

The British Army of the Rhine gave itself up to drinking and wantoning. There is no reason to suppose that the Americans were any better. In France from 1940 to 1944, the German officers and other ranks had not had as a rule the means to betray the dignity of their cloth. But when the well-paid American soldiery were in France, they would lie dead drunk in the Place de la Concorde, or quaff straight from the bottle while occupying more than their share of seats in the crowded civilian trains. They made no distinction among French women, all of whom were fair game for their gross attentions. I have no information on this head from the area of Germany

51

in American occupation, but with women and drink obtainable even more cheaply than in France, what do you suppose? However, it is enough for my purpose to refer you to the behaviour of the troops of our own country. In a statement issued in August 1946, fifteen months after the surrender, the chaplain-general of the British Army of the Rhine said:

A sad proportion of the occupying armies are playing a shameful part in encouraging the rot [of Germany]. Too many are exploiting for financial gain the material needs of this conquered people. Too many are prostituting women and girls.

There were wholesale evictions in order to afford offices, messes, and billets. If we turn to Chapter XIV of the British *Manual of Military Law*, we find that it summarizes the rules and customs of war on land and, in its latter part, deals with the behaviour of an invader in occupied territory. Paragraph No. 412 reads, and there is a similar rule in the corresponding American manual: 'In quartering troops in private dwellings [in occupied territory], the inhabitants should not be driven into the streets without shelter. Rooms are to be left to their use.' You told me, you remember, that when you were posted to the British army in Germany at the end of 1945, you were given a whole apartment for your private quarters. So that you might occupy it, the German tenant was ordered to remove himself into the street at only half an hour's notice, and allowed to take with him no more than a single suitcase. All his rooms and all the rest of his belongings were left for the sole use of one officer— yourself. This treatment thousands of Germans suffered. In a country where countless houses had been either destroyed or rendered uninhabitable by bombing, the overcrowding that resulted rose to incredible heights of insanitary hardship. Yet any pretext served for new evictions. To give but one instance, a whole housing estate was seized in order to serve as a camp for displaced persons.

You may say that, however civilians were treated in the West of Germany, there was at least no deportation of them to slave labour, deportation such as the Germans were pronounced guilty of by the international military tribunal at Nuremberg. That is easily explained. It was prisoners of war that Russia, Britain, and France turned into slave labour.

Little has been learned in Britain and the United States of the lot of prisoners of war in Russia. But that little shows that it evidently varied a good deal. At one extreme there was the show camp of Krasnoyarsk near Moscow. It is there that were detained Field-Marshal von Paulus, former commander of the German sixth army, who surrendered at Stalingrad, and General von Seydlitz. In 1943 the Russians made von Paulus chairman of the Free Germany committee (*Freies Deutschland*), a shadow German government on Russian soil. There was also the Union of German Officers with General von Seydlitz as its president. Very likely the existence of the shadow government at Krasnoyarsk contributed to instilling a fear in the British and United States governments during the war that Russia might conclude a separate peace with Germany, a fear that had a far-reaching effect on their policy. In August 1945 both the Free Germany committee and the Union of German Officers were dissolved, but only to be replaced by a new body, the Military Committee for the Renovation of Germany, the first chairman of which was a German named Einsiedel.

In view of the parts played by Field-Marshal von Paulus and other senior German officers detained at Krasnoyarsk, there is no virtue in their having been cared for like potential Derby winners. At the other extreme were the two million German, Italian, Finnish,

53

and Hungarian prisoners of war who were stated at the end of 1946 to be employed—together with 800,000 Japanese—in the building of a railway from near Kuibyshev on the Volga to Taishev on the Transsiberian, a distance of 2,500 miles.[1] It is not to be supposed that they were particularly well cared for. Indeed, a German soldier who in April 1948 was repatriated from Russia to the area of Germany in French occupation informed the Zürich paper, *Weltwoche*, shortly after his return home, that all technicians—including doctors, electricians, joiners, and workmen familiar with any kind of machinery—were given enough, relatively speaking, to eat, but that prisoners of war without technical training, such as shop assistants, clerks, officials, teachers, and musicians, were put to the heaviest manual labour—road-building, mining, forestry, quarrying—and had to accomplish each day a fairly high norm of this work, to which they were unaccustomed and for which they were ill-fitted, if they were to avoid being punished and having their already meagre food allowance reduced. According to another repatriated German prisoner, in some camps the captives were supplied during the winter with felt boots, fur coats, gloves, caps, and wadded clothing out of Russian army stocks. But it was noticeable that nearly all the German prisoners of war who came home from Russia had nothing but the tatters of their German uniform.

How many could never come home it would be difficult to say. In March 1947, Mr. Molotov, the Russian foreign minister, stated that one million German prisoners of war had been repatriated from Russia, and that only 890,000 remained. If those figures were correct, the mortality among prisoners must have been very high, for it was estimated in January 1947 that Russia must have

[1]*Irkutskaya Pravda*, quoted by United Press message from Shanghai in *New York Times*, 17 December 1946.

captured at least four million German soldiers. And, indeed, concerning prisoners of war of other nationalities detained in Russia, some tens of thousands of Rumanians were not accounted for, and, according to a statement made by the Italian government in February 1947, out of 60,000 Italians known to have been captured only 12,500 had returned home.

What of Germany's western victors?

Britain, France, and the United States, unlike Russia, are signatories of the Geneva convention, an agreement which governs the treatment of prisoners of war. Article 75 of this convention provides that prisoners of war shall be repatriated as speedily as possible after the conclusion of peace, or, in the event of conquest, as soon as a condition of peace is in fact established. No doubt the letter of this article allows it to be contended that conquerors may retain their prisoners till conditions in the conquered country are what they consider peaceful. But surely the real meaning of the article is that as soon as hostilities have ceased, prisoners are to be sent home, unless there is a prospect that hostilities will break out again, and that is something which conquest renders most unlikely.

What, in fact, did Britain, France, and the United States do?

It was on 10 August 1947—twenty-eight months after the end of hostilities—that the last of the German prisoners of war in the American zone of their country were released, and the United States military government there announced at the same time that America was the first belligerent to free all its prisoners of war. Even if a little late, that sounded very fine! But it left out of account that shortly after the German surrender the United States government in Washington undertook to transfer each month to the French authorities a certain number of German prisoners of war in order to provide France with

55

additional labour. Other batches of prisoners were transferred from American to British custody. The bargains provoked the indignation of Cardinal Frings, the archbishop of Cologne. In a letter written in August 1946 to Prince Friedrich of Hohenzollern, he said he wished to protest 'in the name of humanity and justice'

against an infamous trade in human beings. German prisoners of war are brought over from the United States with the hope that at last they are going to see their homeland again and their families, and instead they are delivered into the hands of Britain and France, and put to the most severe kind of forced labour.[1]

These words of the cardinal's express a moral judgement which none can gainsay.

As for the French, in the summer of 1945 the French government announced that it was putting 220,000 German prisoners of war to work, and that it expected *by the end of 1946*—that is to say, twenty months after hostilities had ended—to be employing 1,700,000.[2] However, it did not turn out that way. For one thing, there arose the question of the French treatment of prisoners. In July 1945, the United States government, in accordance with the arrangement that had been made, transferred 320,000 German prisoners to the French. Then, in the following September, the transfers were suspended. The United States military authorities suspended them because, so they stated, both the International Red Cross and the American Red Cross had found the administration of camps for prisoners of war in France unsatisfactory and the German prisoners in them not being properly treated. In particular, the sick were being neglected. So it was that in September 1947—twenty-nine months after the German surrender—the French government was only

[1]*Catholic Herald* (London), 23 August 1946.
[2]*The Times* (London), 18 July 1945.

able to announce that German prisoners in the country then numbered 600,000. The figure did not include any German prisoners that might still have been in the area of Germany in French occupation.

As for Britain, at the end of June 1946 there were 385,000 German prisoners of war in the country, most of them employed in agriculture, on road-mending, or in industry. Thousands of others were detained in Egypt. Regarding those in England, Mr. R. R. Stokes said in the House of Commons in July 1946:[1]

He wished to raise the question of prisoners of war used as slaves. It was obligatory on us to see that the principles of the Geneva Convention were carried out, but the provisions as they affected the treatment of German prisoners of war were being disgracefully dishonoured. . . . When the question of the treatment of prisoners of war was raised in the House of Lords the government answer was sheer buffoonery, and showed incompetence of the worst order. This business of one shilling a day and their keep for prisoners of war was ridiculous. The government were making something like £750,000 a week out of slave labour.

A letter from a German prisoner of war in England, which was published in a weekly newspaper a couple of days after Mr. Stokes spoke, pointed out that the net profit to the British government on each prisoner employed in agricultural work was £2 1s. a week, and on each prisoner employed with a contractor £4 17s. a week.[2]

The last of the German prisoners of war in Britain were not repatriated till after midsummer 1948. But the English are a humane people, and in the previous year there was the petition I have already referred to. On 27 August 1947 the prime minister was led to make a statement. He defended the retention of prisoners of war, not

[1] *The Times* (London), 17 July 1946.
[2] *Catholic Herald* (London), 19 July 1946.

only on the ground that their labour was a form of reparations, but also on the ground that it was required,
'particularly now that our need of agricultural man-power
has so greatly increased'. The reply was deemed unsatisfactory, and on 17 October the joint synod of the Con-
vocation of York adopted a resolution that had been
moved by the archdeacon of Chester (The Ven. R. V. H.
Burne), that the prime minister's reasons for retaining
prisoners of war in England was morally indefensible. As
a result of further agitation, the rate of repatriation was
somewhat accelerated. In the meanwhile, the labour of
prisoners went on being used. Moreover, there was no
suggestion that German prisoners of war would be repatriated from the various countries on the Continent in
which they were being detained in conditions not made
public and there also were being employed as forced
labour.

No doubt in England German prisoners of war were
better treated than in Russia. No doubt in England they
were better treated than in France. No doubt they were,
on the whole, not ill-treated, although in 1945 they were
left many more months than might have been strictly
unavoidable without news of their families, and their living conditions did not invariably tally with the photo-
graphs on the leaflets which the Royal Air Force dropped
among German troops in the fighting line during the
war. But however reasonably they were treated, it is
indisputable that in England, exactly as in Russia, in
France, and elsewhere, they were used as slave labour.

While Germany during the war deported from occupied
territories many thousands of civilians in order to assist
the German war effort, the western victors, once they
were in occupation of Germany, did not deport civilians
in any large number, because, although they no longer
had any war effort to support, they had hundreds of
thousands of prisoners of war in their custody.

Nevertheless, Germans were deported. From the German territories either annexed by Russia or alloted to Poland, and from Czecho-Slovakia, Hungary, and other countries, Germans or persons of Austrian origin or descent were uprooted at short notice out of their age-old homes and deported westward, leaving all their property, except for a few portables, behind. According to Mr. Ernest Bevin, the British foreign secretary, speaking in the House of Commons on 26 October 1945:

Something like four million Germans had left the new Poland down to Stettin; Czecho-Slovakia, Hungary, and other countries added large numbers—probably about four million to four and a half million. That was a total of about nine million.

These deportations or evictions had been approved by Britain and the United States. They were to take place, according to the protocol of the conference of Berlin of July 1945, 'in an orderly and humane manner'. How the decision was complied with you may judge from the following description of a few of the deportees as seen in Berlin:

To-day [a newspaper correspondent wrote][1] I have seen thousands of German civilians—old men and women and children of all ages—reduced to the depths of misery and suffering that the Nazis inflicted on others during their beastly reign. . . .
I saw at the Stettiner Station miserable remnants of humanity, with death already shining out of their eyes—with that awful, wide-eyed stare. Four were dead already, another five or six were lying alongside them, given up as hopeless by the doctor, and just being allowed to die.
The rest sat or lay about, whimpering, crying, or just waiting.

[1]*Daily Herald* (London), 22 August 1945.

59

Later some faint recognition of the claims of humanity was manifested in the mode of deportation, especially from Czecho-Slovakia. But as late as 19 January 1947, the Berlin newspaper *Telegraf* is found describing the deportation of 1,600 Germans in a train despatched from Breslau under the auspices of Polish authorities on 11 December 1946. It arrived at Marienthal, on the border of the British zone in Germany, on 21 December, ten days later. The newspaper's account included the report of a passenger, Frau Gertrude Schmidt. She stated that the deportees were crowded into goods wagons which contained no straw and no stoves, and most of which had not been cleaned. Into each wagon thirty-five persons were packed with all their portable belongings. You and I, who have travelled for a week in a goods wagon with eighteen others, can imagine what this meant. The wagons were closed and not opened till the train reached Kohlfurt on the third day. Frau Schmidt then saw the first dead man. He had been frozen to death. At Kohlfurt the passengers were given their first meal since the train started. It consisted of one loaf of bread among three, a herring among five, some sugar and coffee. Dr. Loch, another passenger, confirmed Frau Schmidt's report, and added that when the train reached Marienthal twelve persons were dead. In a hospital at Rinteln, four more passengers died, and sixteen died between 23 December and 4 January in other hospitals.

On 21 January 1947 another Berlin newspaper stated that the Polish authorities had noticed the cold weather and had postponed further deportations.

As early as February 1946 it was estimated that, following on a war advertised as being waged to bring peace and contentment to mankind, on a war advertised as being waged to bestow on mankind the four freedoms of the Atlantic Charter—including freedom from want and freedom from fear—17 million persons had been evicted from their homes and deprived of their property, and that altogether on the Continent between 25 and 40 million persons were without a roof. But long after February 1946 the deportations went on.

The persons evicted from Poland, Czecho-Slovakia, Hungary, and the areas of Germany annexed by Russia or allotted to Poland, were all sent into the West of Germany. The consequences of the influx you may judge from the fact that in the ruins and rubble of the once-noble city of Cologne, where 30,000 persons were found to be existing precariously in April 1945, there were in August 1946, 510,000 persons. The British military government agreed to receive into the area in its occupation from the Russian zone and from Poland one and a half million persons. But many more came. By the end of 1946 the population of the British zone, where 49 per cent. of the houses had, it was said, been destroyed either by bombing or in the fighting, was, notwithstanding military casualties during the war and the casualties inflicted by bombing, three millions more than in 1939.

Altogether, it is clear that the 'war crimes' of 'murder, ill-treatment, or deportation to slave labour or for any other purpose of civilians of occupied territory' is a 'war crime' with which the victors might be reproached. The international military tribunal at Nuremberg pronounced sixteen of the former German leaders guilty of a 'war crime' of which the victorious powers—by whom the tribunal was set up and whom the judges represented might likewise have been pronounced guilty.

I TURN TO THE SECOND of the six kinds of 'war crime' of which the men in the dock at Nuremberg were pronounced guilty—the 'war crime' of putting inhabitants of occupied territories into concentration camps in order to destroy opposition. It is already clear that the Russian lagiers or corrective labour camps are 'concentration camps'. It is already clear that the thousands deported into Russia from the eastern half of Poland, from the Baltic States, from Bessarabia and Bukovina, and some of those deported from the Russian zone of Germany, were placed in such camps 'in order to destroy opposition'. Moreover, there are, as I write, concentration camps in that part of Germany in Russian occupation.

It was not long before the Russian military government in Germany brought pressure to bear upon members of the Social Democrat party to fuse with the Communists. Local leaders who refused were liable to be sent to a concentration camp. This is what happens in the novel describing life in the Russian zone which I have previously mentioned.[1] Before the story opens, Richard Kunze, the hero, was put into a concentration camp by the German government, because, being a teacher, he was obdurate in his refusal to join the National Socialist party. In order to have work and provide for his family, he has at last accepted party membership. That is to say, he is a nominal National Socialist. Throughout the war, he retains the post he has thus recovered, as he is too old for military service. After the Russians have come, he presently joins the Social Democrats. He is the local chairman. Later the Russians invite him to persuade the branch of Social Democrats to join the Communists. The branch is unanimous in its refusal. So the leaders, including Kunze, are seized as they leave their meeting, and are shipped off to a concentration camp. When they

[1] *Zwischen Braun und Rot.*

get there, Richard Kunze recognizes the gateway. The Russians are putting him in the very concentration camp to which he had been sent by the National Socialists, and for the same reason: his political opinions! Clearly, in this respect, Russian and German National Socialist behaviour were indistinguishable.

Moreover, the alleged 'war crime' of 'destroying opposition' by putting people of occupied territory in concentration camps was committed not only by the Russians, but also by the victorious powers of the West. For with the advent of the western conquerors, internment camps became as abundant in the western zones of Germany as in the eastern zone. In the West they were mainly reserved, it is true, for former members of the German National Socialist party, obdurate men who would not renounce their political beliefs at a foreigner's bidding, but it is indisputable that the object was precisely that with which the former German leaders were reproached at Nuremberg—namely, to destroy, by forestalling, possible opposition.

Of that I shall have more to say later, when I come to 'crimes against humanity'. In the meanwhile, there is the third kind of 'war crime' of which some accused at Nuremberg were pronounced guilty—the 'war crime' of 'murder or ill-treatment of prisoners of war'.

Murder? No doubt by the western belligerents there was no systematic murder of prisoners of war. Yet on the victorious side 'regrettable incidents' had of course occurred. Many British soldiers who served in the Western Desert of North Africa in 1940 have spoken of an ugly incident at Benghazi, when drunken Australians shot up a fair-sized group of disarmed Italians. Such incidents seem unavoidable in the heat of battle, the confusion of retreat, or owing to an opportunity for unchecked sadism. It should not be pretended that they occur on one side only. Here is an extract of one lecture which was given

63

during the war at the British War Office No. 1 School:[1]

Even if it is impossible to take prisoners, you must capture despatch-riders and question them before you 'despatch' them as silently as possible. . . . If you want to despatch an enemy quickly, use a dagger or some kind of 'cosh'. Other useful weapons are 'snub nosed bullets', hammers—either to smash a man's skull or to hit him with between the shoulderblades to stun him—cheese-cutters—the wires with wooden handles you see in the grocery stores—which are handy for strangling people; fish-lines, for strangling too; and a handkerchief with a fistful of sand in it.

In the Indictment presented to the international military tribunal at Nuremberg, there occurred, under the heading 'Murder and Ill-Treatment of Prisoners of War', the allegation that 'American prisoners, officers and men, were murdered in Normandy during the summer of 1944'. The allegation leads a circumspect reader to recall that there has been no avowal or denial of an order issued to the British and American troops that landed in Normandy in 1944 'to take no prisoners'. Of course, prisoners were taken by the invaders in Normandy, but in view of the above allegation it would be of value to know if there were not occasions when, as in the final British offensive of 1918, assault troops were told that it would be impossible to arrange for prisoners to be conducted to the rear. So too regarding the American treatment of prisoners immediately after landing in Sicily in 1943.

If, regarding the accusation of murder of prisoners of war, at least that much has to be said of the western belligerents, how many German prisoners of war, and especially officers, were 'liquidated' in Russia will in all probability never be known. Much was made in the Indictment, and by the prosecution during the trial, and by the tribunal in its Judgement, of the shooting of fifty

[1]Quoted in Major-General J. F. C. Fuller, *Thunderbolts* (1946).

64

officers of the Royal Air Force who had escaped from Stalag Luft III at Sagan during the war and were recaptured. Later the United States authorities held a trial at Dachau of Germans accused of responsibility for the murder of American soldiers at Malmédy. Those were deeds foul enough. Nevertheless, that such deeds were committed by Germans only on a small scale suggests that, in the 'liquidation' of prisoners of war, the Germans, in comparison with the Russians, were mere children.

Under Count Three—War Crimes, Section (C), 'Murder and Ill-Treatment of Prisoners of War', Subsection 2— the Indictment of the former German leaders contained the following statement:

In September 1941, 11,000 Polish officers, who were prisoners of war, were murdered in the Katyn Forest near Smolensk.

Whose prisoners of war were the 11,000 Polish officers was not stated, whether Russia's, Germany's, or even Finland's. It appears, moreover, that in the first draft of the Indictment the number of Polish officers specified was, not 11,000, but 925, and that a correction, making the number '11,000', was added to the Indictment on a separate slip of paper.[1] Over that particular accusation, when it was brought against the 'major war criminals' who were subsequently put into the dock at Nuremberg, there was, evidently, some indecision.

That is not surprising. Various versions of the dark story of the Forest of Katyn have previously appeared in print.[2] All were based on incomplete data. As I have the

[1]Gallieni Gallus, *Nuremberg and After* (Newtown, Montgomeryshire: The Montgomeryshire Printing and Stationery Co., 1946), p. 22.

[2]*Amtliches Material zum Massenmord von Katyn* (Berlin, 1943); *Truth about Katyn: Report of the Soviet Special Commission* (London, 1944); Odette Keun, *Continental Stakes* (1944), pp. 27-9; W. L. White, *Report on the Russians* (1945), pp. 105-10; Gallieni Gallus, *Nuremberg and After*, op. cit., passim.

65

full facts, it may be as well to give them briefly. They are as follows.

On 13 April 1943 the German wireless announced that German troops had unearthed in the Forest of Katyn, not far to the west of Smolensk, mass graves containing thousands of bodies of Polish officers. It accused the Russian government of having had these officers murdered. Two days later, on 15 April, the Soviet information bureau issued a denial of the accusation. It stated that Russians were not implicated. To begin with, the Russian government suggested that the corpses must be the remains of prehistoric men, as such remains had already been found in the neighbourhood. However, as the bodies were in Polish uniform, this first suggestion was discarded in favour of another. The bodies, the Russian information bureau now said, must be those of Polish soldiery murdered by the Germans after the German armies, in the course of their advance into Russia, had occupied the area of Smolensk. September, October, or even August, 1941, was the probable date.

In the clothing on the bodies, in addition to diaries, letters, and small articles like home-made wooden cigarette cases, were identity papers. From these papers names were taken, which the German wireless went on to broadcast. By the Polish government then having its seat in London, and also by Poles in Poland, the names were recognized as being those of some of nearly 15,000 Poles, who had been among the prisoners of war taken by the Russian armies when these invaded Poland on 17 September 1939, but who had disappeared at the end of April and at the beginning of May 1940.

From October or November 1939 till their disappearance, the 15,000 had been distributed in three camps. One camp at Kozyelsk contained about 4,500 Polish officers and cadets, and a second camp at Starobyelsk about 3,900. In the third camp, at Ostashkov, were about

6,500 Polish prisoners of war, some officers, but most of them policemen, gendarmes, or frontier guards. Kozyelsk lies between Smolensk and Tula, south-west of Moscow. Starobyelsk is roughly midway between Kharkhov and Stalingrad. Ostashkov is between Kalinin and the newly risen Volga. All three camps consisted of disused convents.

From Kozyelsk at the end of April 1940 and at the beginning of May, 245 prisoners were transferred to another small camp at Pavlishchev Bor, in the midst of woods between Kozyelsk and Vyasma. They were moved in two parties, the first on 26 April and the second on 12 May. They met there 79 prisoners from Starobyelsk and 124 from Ostashkov. There was thus formed at Pavlishchev Bor a group of 448 Polish prisoners drawn from the three camps (245 plus 79 plus 124), and the group remained there till June, when it was moved to Gryazovetz, just to the south of Vologda. The 448 prisoners were still at Gryazovetz in September 1941—fifteen months later—when the Russian government put that camp—one wing of a disused convent—in charge of the commander of the new Polish army which was then raised in Russia, in accordance with a Russo-Polish military agreement signed in Moscow on the previous 14 August.

Meanwhile, simultaneously with the formation of the small group of 448 prisoners at Pavlishchev Bor, the three camps — Kozyelsk, Starobyelsk, and Ostashkov — were closed. From about 26 April onwards the inmates not included in the small parties were taken away in groups, so many at a time. From Kozyelsk went 4,500 less 245: say, 4,250. From Starobyelsk, 3,900 less 79: say, 3,820. From Ostashkov, 6,500 less 124: say, 6,375. That is to say, in all about 14,445.

At Gryazovetz the group of 448 continued to receive letters from relatives, although the letters were at first addressed to Kozyelsk, Starobyelsk, or Ostashkov, as the case might be, and had to be sent on. But letters to any

of the remaining 14,445 prisoners who had been at one
or another of those three camps were returned to the
senders, the envelopes being stamped by the Russian post
office with the French words: *'Retour—parti.'*

Nevertheless, the Polish government in London did not
yet suspect that anything was amiss, and one day in the
autumn of 1940—while Russia was still the 'ally' of
Germany—a Polish staff officer, Colonel Berling, had a
conversation in the Lubyanka building in Moscow, ad-
jacent to the notorious prison, with Mr. Lavrentli Beria,
then head of the N.K.V.D. and later Russian minister
of the interior. There was also present another N.K.V.D.
official named Merkulov. It was proposed to Colonel
Berling that a Polish division might be raised and incorporated in the Red army. When Colonel Berling
suggested that the Polish officers who had been prisoners
at Kozyelsk and Starobyelsk could serve as cadres for such
a division, Merkulov exclaimed: 'No, no! Not them. We
have made a great blunder about them.'

In the next year, 1941, at the end of July, after Germany
had gone to war with Russia, the Russians and Polish
governments signed in London a treaty of friendship, and
in August this was supplemented by the military agreement to which I have already referred. Under this agreement 45,000 Polish prisoners of war had, by the beginning
of October, reached the collecting points in Russia for
personnel of the new Polish army that it had been decided
to form. General Anders was released from the Lubyanka
prison, and given command of this army. But the 14,445
prisoners of war (officers, policemen, gendarmes, and
frontier guards) who had been at the three camps remained unaccounted for. Accordingly, the Polish government in London—sometimes through its ambassador in
Moscow, Professor S. Kot, sometimes through General
Sikorski and General Anders, sometimes through other
emissaries—applied to the Russian government on eight

68

or nine separate occasions—the first on 6 October 1941, the last on 8 July 1942—to be given the whereabouts of these men; and either from Stalin himself,[1] or from Commissar Molotov and Vice-Commissar Vyshinsky, it elicited only evasive replies. Either the missing prisoners had been released or the missing prisoners had escaped. Perhaps they had escaped to Manchuria. Where or when they were released or they escaped—that was never stated.

As regards the reply that they had been released, it is to be noted that in October 1941 the Polish underground in Warsaw informed the Polish government in London that no prisoner from any of the three camps—Kozyelsk, Starobyelsk, Ostashkov—could be located in Poland or in any German prisoners' camp.

When the German wireless in April 1943 announced the discovery of the mass graves at Katyn, the Russian government's previous uncertainty regarding the fate of the missing Polish prisoners was at once dissipated. Now the Russian government professed to know exactly what had happened to them, not only while they had been in Russian hands, but also, apparently, afterwards. There was no more talk of their having been released. Now the Russian government said that all the time since April 1940 the prisoners had been in three camps near Smolensk —till the German armies overran the area in the summer of 1941. It was the Germans who had murdered them some months later. Oddly enough, when Mr. Maisky, the Russian ambassador in London, had informed the Polish government on 4 July 1941, in the presence of Sir Alexander Cadogan, of the British Foreign Office, of the numbers of Polish prisoners in Russian hands, he had not mentioned the existence of the three camps near Smolensk which the German armies were now alleged to have overrun.

[1] General Sikorski's two conversations with Stalin are given at length in Jan Ciechanowski, *Defeat in Victory* (1947), chaps. VI and VII.

On 17 April 1943, four days after the German wireless had broadcast the discovery of the mass graves at Katyn, the Polish minister of national defence in London announced that his government was asking the International Red Cross at Geneva to hold an inquiry. The German government associated itself with the request. At once the Russian government professed itself indignant. On 20 April the Russian news agency Tass referred to 'Hitler's Polish collaborators', and announced the Russian government's flat refusal to consent to any inquiry by the International Red Cross. On 26 April the Russian government severed diplomatic relations with the Polish government.

Meanwhile, the German government conveyed to Katyn, not only various parties of Poles, a group of foreign newspaper correspondents, a group of German journalists, and small parties of British and American prisoners of war, but also a technical team of the Polish Red Cross. Further, at the request of the German minister of health, an international commission of experts in forensic medicine (the composition of which I shall refer to later) carried out an inquiry at Katyn from 28 to 30 April, and on 4 May its report was published in the German press.

In view of the Russian government's refusal to consent to an inquiry by the International Red Cross, this body declined to intervene. Accordingly, at the end of August 1943, the German government published its own report, entitled *Amtliches Material zum Massenmord von Katyn* (to which I refer henceforth as *Amtliches Material*).

That same autumn the German armies were driven out of the area of Smolensk, and in January 1944 the Russian government conveyed foreign newspaper correspondents to Katyn, so that they might witness a second exhumation. The Russian government also published the result of an inquiry which it conducted on the spot, the English translation of which is entitled *Truth about*

Katyn. The inquiry took place entirely *en famille.* No foreigner, and certainly no Pole, was present. Many of the inhabitants of the locality who gave evidence at this inquiry were those who had testified in 1943 to the Germans, to the Polish Red Cross, and to the international commission of experts in forensic medicine. The second time the evidence was the direct opposite of what the same witnesses had said the first time. Oddly enough, the evidence now tallied perfectly with that version of the affair which the Russian government had suddenly put forward when the German wireless announced the discovery of the graves and accused the Russian government of being responsible for the corpses. The evidence tallied so perfectly that it may be said an inquiry was unnecessary.

On one thing, and on one thing only, *Amtliches Material* (the German report) and *Truth about Katyn* (the Russian report) are agreed. It is that the parties of Polish officers arrived at Gnezdevo station, eight miles west of Smolensk, on a succession of days in April 1940 (the Polish Red Cross established that actually the two last parties arrived on 9 and 10 May). Of course, in *Truth about Katyn* alone is it stated that the prisoners were taken from this station to camps between fifteen and twenty-five miles distant. It would be odd, if this were true, that on a railway line with stations close together, nearer stations were not used for detraining. In *Truth about Katyn* no light is shed on the question. Likewise, there is no mention of the fact that, after being detrained, the Polish officers were placed in batches of about thirty at a time in a single prison omnibus, which each time returned empty in about half an hour. How the omnibus could have done a round trip to the most distant of the camps mentioned—that is to say, a round trip of fifty miles—in half an hour is in *Truth about Katyn* left unexplained.

According to the report of the foreign experts in forensic medicine (which, as I have said, appeared in the German press on 4 May 1943), the cause of death in all the 982 bodies that had been exhumed by 30 April was a bullet wound in the back of the neck. Shooting in the back of the neck is the recognized mode of execution in Russia. It has never been practised in Germany. About one in every five bodies was found to be bound with rope. The testimony of the Polish underground was that the rope was of Russian make. Some of the bodies bore bayonet wounds, and the wounds could only have been inflicted by four-edged bayonets. Such bayonets are peculiar to the Russian army alone.

Elsewhere in the Forest of Katyn at about the same time were found the bodies of Russian civilians executed during the revolution of 1917. Those bodies too all had bullet wounds in the back of the neck.

Over the mass graves of the Poles young spruce trees had been planted. The international commission heard the evidence of a German expert, Forester von Herff. Microscopic examination showed, he said, that these trees were at least five years old, and had been poorly grown in the shade of larger trees. They had been transplanted to the site of the graves three years earlier.

According to the commission's report, the diaries, letters, and newspapers in the clothing on the bodies dated from the autumn of 1939 to March and April 1940. The latest dated item was a Russian newspaper of 22 April 1940. The bodies were in winter clothing—furs, leather jerkins, woollen sweaters, and so on. This is a material fact. If the Poles were executed, as is alleged in *Truth about Katyn*, in August, September, or October, 1941, when the mean temperature in the area of Smolensk is about 65° Fahr., how account for the presence of winter clothing? But if the date of April-May 1940 is accepted, when only the Russians could have carried out the mass executions, the winter clothing is only to be expected; for the mean temperature at that period is 45° Fahr. As Mr. W. L. White remarks in his book,[1] the foreign newspaper correspondents who were taken to Katyn by the Russian government in January 1944, to witness a second exhumation, expressed astonishment that the Poles should be in winter clothing if they were murdered in August or September.

The commission's report also stated that no insects or remains of insects were in the graves. This again is inexplicable if the Poles were executed, as is alleged in *Truth about Katyn*, in the warm weather.

A fact not mentioned in the report of the commission of experts in forensic medicine, but given in *Amtliches Material*, is that German ammunition was evidently used for the executions. There were eight graves. In Grave No. 2 one unused bullet was found. This bullet, it was established, had been manufactured at Burlach near Karlsruhe between 1922 and 1931. Large quantities of such ammunition were exported during some of those years to Poland, the Baltic States, and Russia. In *Truth about Katyn* no use is made against the Germans of the presence of German ammunition in the graves.

Finally, the commission's report declared that there was on the surface of the brain-pulp of a number of bodies examined a calcareous incrustation such as is only observed in corpses that have been buried for at least three years.

The members of the commission of experts in forensic medicine numbered twelve. All but one were, naturally, from countries then allied with Germany or else from occupied territories. All twelve signed the report. Among them was Professor Marko Markov, then professor of forensic medicine in the University of Sofia.

[1] Loc. cit.

At this point we may see what happened at the Nuremberg Trial. In the Indictment, as I have said, it was asserted that 11,000 Polish prisoners of war had been executed at Katyn. At the instance of one of the accused, Hermann Goering, more than a day of the trial was allotted, at the beginning of July 1946, to hearing evidence for and against this accusation. The only member of the international commission called as a witness was Professor Markov. 'Readily', so it was reported, he went back on the opinion which he had expressed in signing the report published on 4 May 1943. 'Readily' his change of mind may be explained. In the interval Bulgaria had passed from dependence on Germany to dependence on Russia.

But if he changed his mind, another signatory of the report did not change his. As I have said, there was among the twelve experts an exception, one who was from a country neither allied with Germany nor in German occupation. He was a neutral. He was a Swiss. He was Dr. F. Naville, who was then and, as I write, is still, professor of forensic medicine in the University of Geneva. Unlike Professor Markov, he is still free to say exactly what he believes to be true. Owing to his having signed the report, he was threatened in 1945 with proceedings, but he was not to be intimidated. He stood his ground. And of course the threat proved empty. I have questioned him.

He tells me that he stands by every word of the unanimous report to which he put his signature at Smolensk on 30 April 1943. In his mind there is no doubt whatever regarding who executed the Polish prisoners of war.

If we really wish to understand the meaning of the Nuremberg Trial, we must bear in mind that he was not called as a witness at that Trial.

The tribunal had the opportunity of hearing an independent opinion. It did not take it. No wonder the

74

correspondent ot *The Times* was led to report:[1] 'The attempt by Goering's counsel to establish that the crime was not committed by the Germans can hardly be said to have prospered.' However, in a book which this newspaper correspondent published in the following year, he took another view. He then wrote:[2]

It cannot be said that the evidence at Nuremberg carried the matter much further: both sides produced their witnesses and affidavits and one had the impression that the last word had not been heard.

The last word had not. Even here, in this letter, there is more that has to be said.

As I have mentioned, there were found at Katyn eight mass graves. Seven are grouped close together. The eighth is about a hundred yards away from the others, lower down the shelving, boggy ground and nearer to the River Dnieper. It was not unearthed till some time after the others. In this eighth grave the latest newspaper was dated '6 May 1940', and in fact the last two parties of Polish officers are known to have left the camp at Kozyelsk for Gnezdevo station on 9 and 10 May 1940. According to *Amtliches Material*, the total number of bodies exhumed from the seven graves was 4,143. The figure was confirmed by the technical team of the Polish Red Cross. In view of the size of the eighth grave, it cannot have contained more than about 110 bodies. That makes the total of Polish prisoners of war excuted at Katyn 4,253.

It is obvious that whoever inserted in the Nuremberg Indictment the accusation that Germans had been guilty of the executions did not know this. As I have said, in

[1] *The Times* (London), 2 July 1946.
[2] R. W. Cooper, *The Nuremberg Trial* (Penguin Books, No. 598), p. 43.

the Indictment that number was first put at 925, and
then, on a slip of paper, the figure '11,000' was substituted.
Both figures were equally wide of the mark. What is the
explanation?

When the German wireless first announced the discovery of the graves—in a broadcast on 13 April 1943—
it spoke of 10,000 and even of 12,000 bodies. That was
of course because the German ministry of propaganda
knew that some thousands of Polish prisoners of war
were missing, but not even approximately how many.
The amended figure of 11,000 put into the Nuremberg
Indictment was presumably arrived at as being the mean
of 10,000–12,000. The chief Russian prosecutor, Lieutenant-General R. Rudenko,[1] when in February 1946,
in the course of the trial, he referred to the accusation,
was roughly correct so far as the number of missing goes;
for he spoke of a figure of 15,000. But he too was hopelessly out regarding the number of bodies found at Katyn.

The fact that no more than 4,253 bodies could be
found at Katyn embarrassed the German government,
and on 3 June 1943 it announced that 'exhumation was
being suspended during the summer heat wave'. The
announcement seems to have been made in order to
avoid having to admit that all eight graves had been
emptied and yet that they would not yield either 10,000
or 12,000 corpses.

The question remains: Whence came those 4,253 Polish
officers? As is stated in the report of the experts in forensic
medicine, and as is repeated in *Amtliches Material*, many
of the wooden cigarette cases and other home-made
little articles in the clothing on the bodies had been

[1] I may mention here that while the chief Russian prosecutor at
Nuremberg was a lieutenant-general, the senior of the two
Russian judges was only a major-general. Evidently the Russian
government realized that at the Trial the prosecution was more
important than the bench.

inscribed: 'Kozyelsk 1940'. A fact omitted from the commission's report (perhaps because not known till later), and likewise suppressed in *Amtliches Material*, is that among the bodies found was one, and only one, of a woman. In the camp at Kozyelsk too there had been one Polish woman, and one only—a flight lieutenant. The Polish officers confined in the disused convent at Kozyelsk— less the 245 removed to Pavlishchev Bor—numbered about 4,250, almost exactly the number of bodies unearthed at Katyn. Of those bodies—about 4,253—2,914 were identified. The names on the identity papers in their clothing are given in *Amtliches Material*. Nearly all are names of officers known to have been at Kozyelsk. Not all, because the Polish authorities had not a complete list. There can be no doubt that the bodies unearthed at Katyn were those Polish officers who had been prisoners of war in Russian hands at Kozyelsk till the end of April or the beginning of May 1940.

That leaves about 10,200 Polish prisoners—those who were confined either at Starobyelsk or at Ostashkoy— still unaccounted for; for those too disappeared at the same time. Their fate remains unkown, but it can be surmised. For it is known that the 3,470 prisoners of war at Starobyelsk were taken by train to Kharkhov and there put into lorries, after which there is no trace of them. It is known too that the 6,375 prisoners at Ostashkoy were taken by train to Vyasma and detrained, after which of them also all trace ceases. Perhaps other mass graves in addition to those at Katyn, but not yet unearthed, are to be sought outside Kharkhov and outside Vyasma.

Those are the facts about Katyn. It might seem that from them only one conclusion was to be drawn. The international military tribunal, in its Judgement, did not draw that conclusion. The omission was not due to ignorance. All the information was in its hands. The information, complete in every detail, was sent to Nuremberg in the form of a book of about four hundred foolscap pages produced on a duplicator. The book was entitled *Facts and Documents concerning Polish Prisoners of War Captured by the U.S.S.R. in the 1939 Campaign.* No use of the information was made during the Trial. I do not suggest, however, that the information was ignored. Perhaps it was because the tribunal had received the book that, on the subject of Katyn, it had, in its Judgement, not a word to say.

But that silence was not enough. Previously we have seen, as regards the accusation and conviction of the former German leaders of the 'war crimes' of 'murder, ill-treatment, or deportation of civilians of occupied territory', and of the utilization of concentration camps to destroy opposition in occupied territory, that those crimes were *of a kind* which the victors, who at Nuremberg were both prosecutors and judges, had committed also. Now we have something else. The former German leaders were accused of a particular 'war crime', not only of which no German was guilty, but for which there is no doubt that one of the powers conducting the prosecution and represented on the bench was actually responsible. Yet although this was known to the tribunal, there was no attempt at exoneration. How, then, can we believe that the Trial of the so-called 'major war criminals' was inspired by any desire to extend the dominion of justice? How, then, can ordinary people like you and me avoid wondering if some other charges in the Indictment, charges of which the so-called 'major war criminals' were convicted, were not charges equally dubious?

AMONG THE ACCUSATIONS catalogued in the Indictment, it was not only this one, that 'in September 1941, 11,000 Polish officers, who were prisoners of war, were murdered in the Katyn Forest near Smolensk', that the international military tribunal, in its Judgement, passed over in silence. There were others. It would seem, therefore, that the framing of the Indictment was not invariably guided by strict scruple.

Apart from that, the ill-treatment of prisoners of war was another kind of 'war crime' of which the western victors accused the vanquished when they too had been guilty of it. As regards the French, we have already seen that in September 1945 the United States military authorities suspended the transfer of German prisoners of war to the French, because, so they stated, the French were not treating their prisoners properly. I may be told that the German ill-treatment of prisoners of war and the French ill-treatment are not to be compared, and that the German was much worse. That is as it may be. I should like to be shown the article of the Geneva convention that specifies that some kinds of ill-treatment are permissible, others not. The Geneva convention was posted in every camp which you and I occupied in Germany. We know that there is no such article. It is ill-treatment without qualification that the signatories of the convention renounced.

As for the British, in order to be as brief as possible, let me not dwell on the binding of prisoners at Dieppe in 1942, a matter that led to the British inmates of certain camps in Germany being manacled as a reprisal. Let me not dwell on the causes of the mutiny of German prisoners in a camp in Canada during that same year. Let me go back no further than 1944. Were the interrogation methods then employed at Devizes any less cruel than methods used by the Germans? The same methods were in vogue also in 1944 and 1945 at the London cage. What happened when the British 21 Army group penetrated into Germany? According to the Canadian military newspaper, *Maple Leaf*, when Josef Kramer, commandant of the notorious Belsen camp, arrived at Brussels,

After getting out of a plane which brought him from Germany, he was put in a truck and taken across the airfield. He was slow in getting out of the truck. So a military policeman grabbed him by the back of the neck and threw him out, and he landed on his face in the dirt, whimpering like a child. He presented a sorry sight.[1]

Mr. Leonard O. Mosley, from whom I take the quotation, was at Belsen in April 1945 at the time the place was put under a British guard.

The British soldiers [he says][2] . . . beat the S.S. guards and set them to collecting the bodies of the dead, keeping them always at the double. . . . When one of them dropped to the ground with exhaustion, he was beaten with a rifle-butt. When another stopped for a break, he was kicked until he ran again, or prodded with a bayonet, to the accompaniment of lewd shouts and laughs. When one tried to escape, or disobeyed an order, he was shot. . . . The punishment [these guards] got was in the best Nazi tradition, and few of them survived it.

Mr. Alan Moorehead, the *Daily Express* correspondent, reached Belsen a few days later. Here is part of his account:[3]

As we approached the cells of the S.S. guards the sergeant's language became ferocious.
'We have had an interrogation this morning', the captain said. 'I'm afraid they are not a pretty sight.'
'Who does the interrogation?'

[1]Quoted in Leonard O. Mosley, *Report from Germany* (1945), p. 93 n.
[2]*Report from Germany*, pp. 93-4.
[3]*Eclipse* (1945), pp. 223-4.

'A Frenchman. I believe he was sent up here specially from the French underground to do the job.'

The sergeant unbolted the first door and flung it back with a crack like thunder. He strode into the cell jabbing a metal spike in front of him. 'Get up', he shouted. 'Get up; get up, you dirty bastards.'

There were half a dozen men lying or half-lying on the floor. One or two were able to pull themselves erect at once. The man nearest me, his shirt and face spattered with blood, made two attempts before he got on to his knees and then gradually on to his feet. He stood with his arms half stretched out in front of him trembling violently.

'Get up', shouted the sergeant. They were all on their feet now, but supporting themselves against the wall. 'Get away from that wall.'

They pushed themselves out into space and stood there swaying. Unlike the women they looked not at us but vacantly in front, staring at nothing.

Same thing in the next cell, and the next, where the men, who were bleeding and very dirty, were moaning something in German.

'You had better see the doctor', the captain said. 'He's a nice specimen. He invented some of the tortures here. . . .'

The doctor had a cell to himself.

'Come on. Get up', the sergeant shouted. The man was lying in his blood on the floor, a massive figure with a heavy head and a bedraggled beard. He placed his two arms on to the seat of a wooden chair, gave himself a heave and got half-upright. One more heave and he was on his feet. He flung wide his arms towards us.

'Why don't you kill me?' he whispered. 'Why don't you kill me? I can't stand any more.'

The same phrases dribbled out of his lips over and over again.

Incidentally, at Lüneburg, at the trial in 1945 of Kramer and the rest of the Belsen staff as 'war criminals', the judge advocate stated that this doctor, Klein—one of those sentenced to death and later executed—was not charged with 'deliberate acts of cruelty'.

81

More than a year after the fighting had finished, and while the Nuremberg Trial was going on, two English newspapers reported that during the winter some British camps in Belgium for German prisoners of war had been notorious for shortage of food, brutality, disease, and the organized theft of personal possessions by the guards. A week after this disclosure it was reported by one of the two newspapers that conditions in four camps in which German civilians were interned near Paderborn, in the British area of occupation of Germany, were very bad. The newspaper stated that in one camp five hundred of the 1,500 inmates detained without 'judicial process' had been found in the previous January 1946 to need an enriched diet if they were to survive.

A few days later Mr. Michael Astor asked a question in the House of Commons about both the camps for prisoners of war in Belgium and the camps near Paderborn for civilian internees. The written reply given by the finance member of the Army Council was described by one of the two newspapers which had first raised the matter as bearing 'the too-familiar stamp of the official answer to a disagreeable question'. Both newspapers demanded a public inquiry. There the matter seemed to rest

There the matter rested, except in the memories of the Germans who had suffered. 'Camps No. 2227 and No. 2228', a German prisoner of war then in England stated in October 1947, 'will never be forgotten by thousands.'

In 1947, more than two years after the end of the war, the treatment of prisoners and the interrogation methods employed in a camp at Bad Nenndorf in the British zone of Germany led in the following year to a number of courts-martial At one of these the accu ed, who had been the camp medical officer, stated in evidence that he had been told by the commandant not to put internees in the camp hospital or to use medical equipment for them.[1] At another court-martial a witness called by the prosecution testified to the normal practice in such camps. He said that it was 'quite proper' for a British intelligence officer to tell a former colonel of the S.S., who was suspected of plotting a rising, that his family would be killed. After stating that a man 'would be interrogated till he was broken', the witness added that, if this did not succeed,

> The man would be told that the secret service knows everything about the plot, and that only a complete confession can save his wife and daughter, who are in our hands. If this fails, the man would be put under extreme pressure.

Thanks to the courts-martial, the practices in British interrogation camps in Germany became common knowledge in England. It became known that it was usual for unconvicted suspects to have their clothes taken from them and to be left naked in an unheated cell in the cold weather, to have buckets of cold water thrown over them, and to have a scrubbing-brush flung at them and to be made to scrub the floor of the cell again and again.

Nor was it only prisoners of war or members of the S.S. who might suffer. In April 1948 Mr. T. Driberg, the member for Maldon, drew attention in the House of Commons to the case of a young German, Werner Kleindienst. His politics, past, present, or future, were not in question. He had taken part in the harvest celebration at a German club in a small town in the province of Hanover in October 1947. Some British soldiers, who were, Mr. Driberg said, probably a bit drunk, tried to get into this private celebration, and several persons were injured in the brawl that followed. Later some British officers came to make inquiries. Kleindienst acted as interpreter. His statement was taken, and everything

[1]*Daily Express* (London), 8 April 1948.

seemed all right. But at midnight, two days later, he was sent for again. This time his interrogation began at 2.30 in the morning. He was hit hard in the face repeatedly, and then he was beaten with rubber truncheons on his ribs, where he had been severely wounded in the war. When he told his interrogators this, they made him take off a heavy waterproof. This went on, Mr. Driberg said, till the unfortunate youth made a statement, which he later withdrew, implicating innocent Germans. The interrogation went on till 5.15 a.m., and he was not allowed to go home till nine o'clock the following night.

In reply, the British under-secretary for war said that there had been an error of judgement.

Of course, if our English tradition of judicial decency were not still strong among us even in what may be its death-throes, that such means were being employed to obtain evidence from Germans would never have become known. It would not have been permitted to mention a case in Parliament. Courts-martial, if they took place at all, would be held in camera. And no doubt it is a great deal that publicity—the guarantee against abuse of power—has not yet been forbidden completely.

Even so, the important thing, if we care for fairness and right, is surely not that the happenings become known afterwards, but that they are effectively forestalled. Can you suppose that those means of extorting confessions would have been adopted if it had not been thought that they could be used with impunity, if they had not been tacitly encouraged in advance? The means were used because it was thought that knowledge of their use would not get about. And we should be accepting a too easy comfort if we believed that, behind the few scandals brought to light, there did not lurk others more numerous that remained secret. For, as I shall show in due course, the torture of suspects in order to extort confessions was implicit from the first in the business of prosecuting so-called 'war criminals'.

For the moment, my point is simply that in accusing and convicting individuals among the vanquished of ill-treating prisoners of war and others, the western victors were accusing and convicting them of that which they did themselves. You now know that the French ill-treated prisoners of war. You now know that the English ill-treated them. It is time to mention the Americans.

You have told me how on the eve of the liberation of your prisoners-of-war camp in Germany the senior British officer gave the German officers who were your custodians a chit which they might show to the American troops about to take them prisoner and release you, as evidence that they had behaved decently to you all, and how, when the American spearhead turned up, you realized that the chit had little likelihood of doing any good. It was the same as regards the commandant of the camp for senior British officers, a colonel who had been the soul of punctilious courtesy. When the senior officers spoke to their deliverers in his favour, 'Aw, shucks!' was the reply. 'You don't know what the Germans did to our boys in the Ardennes. We gotta be tough.' Elsewhere too, British officers were shocked at the brutality with which the American army treated the disarmed German soldiers in their power. Whatever had happened in the Ardennes was to be the subject of a trial at Dachau; the Germans alleged to have been guilty were going to be punished. That did not matter. In the meanwhile, like the innocent lamb in Aesop's fable, any German soldier who fell into American hands had to suffer.

Perhaps the most eloquent instance of what capture by Americans meant was that of one who was neither a German nor an Italian. As Mr. Ezra Pound had not set foot in the United States for years before the end of the

85

war, presumably he had by then lost his American citizenship. He is, however, an American by birth. He was known to have broadcast from Rome under the auspices of the Italian government. Whether or not he was guilty of any crime under American law will now never be known. On 13 February 1946 a jury in the United States found him insane and unfit to plead. He was placed in an asylum. That he was found insane is not surprising.

In May 1945 he was living with his family in the hills above Rapallo. He saw an American negro soldier advancing with the native *partigiani* of the locality. He went up to him and asked to be taken to an American command post. This was at Lavagna; from Lavagna he was sent to Genoa as a political prisoner. 'If I ain't worth more alive than dead', he is reported as saying, 'that's that. If a man isn't willing to take some risk for his opinions, either his opinions are no good or he's no good.' That was his last public utterance. After some weeks in detention he was handcuffed and removed by military police in a jeep. He believed that he was on his way to an aerodrome for a flight to the United States. Instead, he was taken to an American military prison at Pisa.

There he was placed in the yard inside a barbed-wire compound with a concrete floor, specially built for him. He had no shelter and no bed, no furniture of any kind. He had no exercise; he was allowed nothing to read. He was allowed to receive letters, but not to write them. He could learn nothing of the fate of his wife and mother. By day he was exposed to the broiling sun; by night he was under the glare of spotlights. He remained in the compound for six or seven weeks. He was sixty years old. He lost his memory, and became a prey to hysterical fears. At the end of six or seven weeks he was given some medical attention, and five months after his arrest he was allowed to communicate with his family.

If that was how American troops treated one of their own countrymen, it goes without saying that Germans taken into their clutches were apt to fare worse. In the trials that followed, the primary object was clearly not to do justice but to secure convictions. For the trial of a group of persons together, it was apparently by no means uncommon for one accused to be singled out and invited to testify against his or her companions on the promise of a prompt release. In at least one case at Dachau, of which particulars are before me, the promise was duly honoured. Where no accused was available to give rein to his imagination in king's evidence, the prosecution might fortify its indictments by other means. For instance, in 1945, members of the S.S., even of inferior rank, were expected to confess their guilt in advance of their trial. It mattered nothing that the international military tribunal had not yet declared membership of the S.S. to be 'criminal'. Anything they might wish to say in their defence or to their credit was ruled out.

On arrival in prison, they were not only relieved—as happens in all prisons—of their money, tobacco, and small personal possessions, but also of a blanket if they brought one, and of any food. They were put into a solitary cell, without paillasse or blanket. Food parcels sent in by relatives were confiscated.

Soon interrogations began. They were of three kinds. The first kind was a straightforward matter of question and answer. If, however, the result of an interrogation of this kind was not what the investigator was bent on obtaining, one of the second kind followed, it might be forthwith. A suspect was made to remove his coat and shirt, and to pass his hands inside his belt or inside the top of his trousers. His arms were then strapped to his body. He was told to stand to attention in the middle of the floor space. An American soldier was stationed on either side of him, and a third faced his back. The

87

investigator sat at a table, and ordered him to answer 'yes' or 'no'. Each time he failed to reply, or replied the opposite of what was expected of him, the American soldier on one side of him would strike him in the bare stomach with the edge of his hand while the soldier on the other side kicked him. He was thereby thrown off his balance, and as he swayed backwards the soldier behind fetched him a crack on the back of the head. The effect of this was to push him towards the upright again, and as this happened he was struck in the face. In this style questioning went on for, perhaps, two hours at a stretch.

A suspect was then conducted back to his bare cell, his face bloody, his eyes blackened and half-closed, his mouth so tumefied that he could hardly open it to drink, his bruised lower jaw making him incapable of biting his small lump of bread, his body red and blue. So long as no 'confession' was forthcoming, suspects were kept on bread and water. They were allowed to wash only every other day, and they were not allowed to shave.

The third kind of interrogation commonly took place in an underground cell. Several such interrogations might go on at the same time, and a German policeman wearing a white armband was stationed on the stairs in order to prevent anybody from coming down and hearing in the passage the cries and moans audible from behind several of a row of closed doors. This third kind of interrogation usually went on till a suspect had become unconscious.

Once a suspect had 'confessed', he was promised hot food and a blanket. In fact, he might not be given a blanket; he might be left to discover his own next time he went to the washroom where it had been placed; his own—that is to say, the blanket that had been taken from him on arrival. As for the hot food, that might be forgotten too.

It was useless for a suspect later on to withdraw his 'confession' and to say that it had been obtained from him under duress. The 'confession' figured as the principal evidence at his trial, and sentence was pronounced on the strength of it.

Nor was it only while in prison awaiting or undergoing interrogation that German suspects in American hands were 'ill-treated'. The inmates of internment camp No. 17 were sleeping in November 1945 in bell tents on the bare frozen earth without a blanket, five men to a tent, too many for comfort, too few for warmth. Of course, for none of them had there been as yet any 'judicial process'. I shall not pause to dwell on all the petty persecution that went on, such as making the suspects, for the possessions of which they had been despoiled, sign a receipt in English—a language which, as a rule, they did not understand—and with the American sergeant or corporal, to make doubly sure, hiding the text with his capacious hand.

To begin with, the German public in general and prominent Germans in particular naturally knew nothing of these happenings. But as the years went by and the prosecution and punishment of so-called 'war criminals' went drearily on, the facts began to leak out. In the summer of 1948 even German newspapers appearing in the American zone—restricted as they were in accordance with those democratic principles of which we have heard so much—printed the abundant rumours that were current, of how, in the American trials of so-called 'war criminals' at Dachau, both the accused and the witnesses had had 'confessions' or else testimony extorted from them. There were forthright public protests, notably by the bishop of Württemberg-Baden, Dr. Theophil Wurm, and later by Monsignor Neuhaeusler.

As I have said, the United States army had charge of all the arrangements for the trial before the international military tribunal at Nuremberg. The so-called 'major war criminals' were, from the first, in the care of this army. How were they treated? As a rule, since at least the Renaissance, men who lost eminent position and were placed in confinement have been treated with some regard to their fallen glory. That was according to a code of manners which the Americans evidently did not recognize. For months before the Trial began, the accused were detained in camps the names of which speak for themselves. The camps were officially named Ashcan and Dustbin. There the accused were treated as if they were already convicted criminals. Indeed, some fared even worse. On 26 April 1946, during the Trial, one of the men in the dock, Julius Streicher, stated in evidence that after being taken into custody he was kept for four days in a cell without clothes.

I was made to kiss negroes' feet. I was whipped. I had to drink saliva. My mouth was forced open with a piece of wood, and then I was spat on. When I asked for a drink of water, I was taken to a latrine and told 'Drink'.[1]

At Nuremberg itself the accused were lodged in bare cells, and at first were not allowed any artificial light. Later, special safety lamps were installed. Each morning each prisoner, including the three subsequently acquitted, had to sweep out his cell. There was no privacy. A guard passed the open grill in the door of each cell every thirty seconds. The food was deliberately kept frugal and was supplied in army mess-tins. One English newspaper pointed out that the cells contained no receptacle for garbage. The reason was, it explained, that there was no garbage to throw away. The accused were given so little to eat that they ate it all. Once the Trial had begun there were, at times when the court was not sitting, the

[1] *The Times* (London), 27 July 1946.

melodramatic alarms and the sudden doubling of the guards. In court, the accused were subjected day after day and hour by hour to the glare of the spotlights. Early in January 1946 Dr. Schacht, who was to be one of the acquitted, was sitting in his cell in his fur coat, for the cell was unheated. As for the prurience of which the accused were constantly the victims, not only on the part of newspaper men, photographers, and caricaturists, but also on the part of psychologists, temperature takers, drug administrators, and their like, it may be said that man's inhumanity to man reached new heights of theatricality; and Louis XI of France, who could think of nothing more ingenious than to shut up his enemies in cages, must from the shades have gnashed his teeth in envy.

Finally, as regards the treatment of prisoners, there were the Russians, whose behaviour it would be discourteous to ignore. In the late summer of 1947 Messrs. Victor Gollancz and R. R. Stokes, visiting Germany together, saw a number of German soldiers repatriated from captivity in Russian hands. Mr. Gollancz spoke to individuals. He went to a camp at Uelzen, about two-hours' drive from Hanover. There he saw five young men.

Heinz K——, Mr. Gollancz says, was a six-foot skeleton. His story was that for a couple of years he had been one of 1,200 German prisoners of war at Kharkhov. Every week eight to twelve of them died. That was where he himself became a skeleton. From Kharkhov he was sent to Dresden. There every unmarried German between the ages of seventeen and forty-five had to register. Shortly afterwards he was at a uranium mine at Johanngeorgenstadt in the Erzgebirge. The food was worse than at Kharkhov. He worked underground for eight and a half hours a day seven days a week, loading wagons and holding the drill by arrangement with a friend, as he was too weak to be a 'striker'.

Hans N—— was a prisoner of war at Kiev till December 1946. He worked in a coalmine, and was released 'because he was under-nourished'. From 3 February to 25 July 1947 he was in a Russian prison at 22, Porsestrasse, Magdeburg. A strong light glared in his cell night and day. Three times every twenty-four hours he was questioned for two hours at a time by a Russian officer, who brandished a revolver. He was asked such questions as: 'Why did you fight against the Russians?' 'How many did you kill?' This went on for two or three days; then, after a pause, it started all over again. He was subjected to this treatment, it turned out, because he belonged to the Waffen S.S. He escaped from Magdeburg and reached the British zone.

A young man whose name Mr. Gollancz does not give told him, he says, a muddled story of how he had been on parole from a prison or prison camp and had seen his wife, mother, and child put against a wall and shot in that part of Germany given over to Poland. He was half-mad, Mr. Gollancz says, and his story did not make sense. The official of the Control Commission who was present said that stories of the kind might be exaggerated, but they were very numerous.

Rudolf M—— was twenty-two. A native of Silesia, he was taken prisoner by the Russians in East Prussia in March 1945 and sent to a prisoners-of-war camp in the Urals which had 30,000 inmates. He was put to work in a tank factory for ten hours a day seven days a week. Incidentally, when the international military tribunal at Nuremberg delivered its Judgement, it was the principal Russian judge, Major-General I. T. Nikit-chenko, who read that part of the Judgement in which Article No. 52 of the Hague Rules for War on Land was quoted. According to this rule, citizens of an invaded country are not to be obliged 'to take part in military operations against their own country'. He went on to speak of deportees from German-occupied territories who were made to assist the German war effort. But what was work in a Russian tank factory if not of military importance? To go on with Rudolf M——, on 5 August 1947 he was brought to Frankfurt-on-the-Oder and told that he was going to a rest camp, but he discovered that he was being drafted to a uranium mine in Saxony. He escaped barefooted.

Worst of all, Mr. Gollancz says, was Werner M——, who was twenty-eight and looked seventy. He was in the German Red Cross and was taken prisoner by the Russians at Briansk in February 1943. He was made to work for a month in the Russian front line. Then he was sent to the lead and copper mines in the Urals. He was at the same camp as Rudolf M——. He worked in the mine for two years, and carried on for another two. The mine had no mechanical equipment. He worked for ten hours a day seven days a week. He had to carry a load of 80 lb. in a wicker basket on his back, up a ladder from ledge to ledge. He made four journeys, up and down, every day. He was covered with sores and had water on the knee, owing to malnutrition.

Mr. Gollancz saw individuals. Mr. Stokes saw German prisoners of war returning from captivity in Russian hands in the mass. He was at Friedland near Göttingen on 25 August 1947 when shortly before nine o'clock in the morning the transfer of a party of repatriated prisoners of war from the Russian to the British zone began. This is his description:[1]

At one mile an hour they came, a grey, dirty mass of diseased humanity, looking more like animals than men, led by several rows of men on crutches—not from wounds, but from hunger and accidents. . . . A more emaciated, starved, bedraggled crowd I have never seen in all my experience of displaced

[1] *Manchester Guardian*, 22 September 1947.

persons, prisoners of war, and the like. Practically none of them had proper boots, some were barefooted, some had slippers or rags wrapped round their feet. Lame, on crutches, and sick alike, they had to walk the eight kilometres from the station. . . . About 1,300 prisoners of war came over in all. . . . Later the doctor took me round and showed me the worst cases, one of which I had photographed—a human wreck, one-third of his normal weight and nothing but skin and bone. So far twenty-five per cent. of the men returned suffer badly from hunger oedema, two-thirds of the remainder had obvious signs of prolonged under-nourishment and overwork, and about five per cent. only were capable of doing a day's work.

THE NEXT KIND of 'war crime', after 'murder and ill-treatment of prisoners of war', to be imputed to the former German leaders at the Trial was the 'shooting of hostages'. For hostages to be taken and likewise for some of them to be shot certain circumstances are required. An army has to have occupied enemy territory and the security of this army has then either to be actually threatened or else to be thought in danger. Hence during the greater part of the period of fighting the occasion for taking and *a fortiori* for shooting hostages was denied to the ultimate victors. But once Germany had been invaded the Russians in particular may be said to have made up for lost time. They did not invariably restrict themselves to selecting their hostages from among adults. In the German schools of the Russian zone as well as in other official places the display of a large portrait of Stalin on the wall was obligatory. Supposing such a portrait in a schoolroom to be defaced by the addition of, say, a beard, and supposing a Russian official to discover the fact, the culprit would be invited to disclose himself, and in the event no culprit came forward, hostages from among the school-children would be taken. It would be announced that if the culprit had not come forward within forty-eight hours those hostages would be shot. If, then, a boy, in order to save his companions, did declare himself guilty, he would be promptly executed, but the remaining children would not be released. As likely as not, they would be deported to Russia.[1]

Furthermore, the last thing that ought to be assumed is that the Russians were the villains of the piece in Germany, and that the taking of hostages, for example, was a procedure peculiar to them alone. As we have seen, at courts-martial of British officers in the British zone of occupation it was stated in evidence that when a German political suspect was being interrogated and he did not vouchsafe all that was expected of him, he would be told that his wife and family were in British custody and that they might be made to suffer on his account; that is to say, wife and family would be hostages. This evidence was not questioned at the court-martial.

Invariably the safety of the armies of occupation was the essential factor. As soon as the inhabitants of the western zones had more or less settled down, a British or American officer could drive about entirely by himself and run no danger. But when the French army of liberation occupied Alsace in 1944, and many Germans were still residing there, it happened that French soldiers alone or in pairs were sometimes attacked in lonely places. At the beginning of December General Leclerc, the French commander, did not hesitate to announce that for every French soldier killed by isolated and covert attack he would shoot five hostages.

[1] Cf. *Zwischen Braun und Rot*, op. cit.

THE FIFTH KIND of 'war crime' of which former German leaders were accused and convicted at Nuremberg was 'plunder of public and private property' in occupied territories. In the Indictment the so-called 'defendants' were alleged to have 'ruthlessly exploited the people and the material resources of the countries they occupied', and the international military tribunal, in its Judgement, pronounced that the evidence had established the allegation. Both in the Indictment and in the Judgement, the accusation was subdivided under six heads, as follows:

1) Seizure of works of art and of other 'cultural valuables';

2) Degradation of the standard of life of the civilian population;

3) Seizure of raw materials and of industrial machinery;

4) Confiscation of businesses, plants, and other property;

5) Direction of the resources and production of the occupied countries;

6) Abrogation of the rights of the occupied peoples to develop and to manage agricultural and industrial properties.

As regards this kind of 'war crime', it is impossible to suppose, in the first place, that all works of art and—to adopt the curious but comprehensive term used in the Indictment—other 'cultural valuables' were respected by the victors in occupied Germany, or that German private property wherever it might be was held inviolate unless it was indispensable to the needs of the occupying armies. According to the Indictment, the accused, in being guilty of this fifth kind of 'war crime', had infringed Nos. 46 to 56 of the Hague Rules of 1907. No. 52 of those rules is that private personal property not susceptible of direct military use must not be taken in an occupied country except when it is actually needed for the army. When

Princess Elizabeth and the Duke of Edinburgh visited Paris in May 1948 they were entertained by the president of the French Republic at a state dinner in his official residence, the Elysée. The dinner service used for the occasion consisted of seven hundred pieces of massive plate, which had been ordered and, it was stated, *paid for* by a private German customer during the German occupation of France.[1] The service cannot have been seized by the French government because it was required for the needs of the French army in Germany, and the odd thing is that the French government should have boasted of such an acquisition. I am reminded of the Frenchman whose voice vibrated with indignation as he told the story, possibly apocryphal, that the Duke of Wellington, while at Paris in 1815, went to the Louvre and shied up a ladder in order to take down with his own hands pictures that were transferred to London. For if there was any mote in the Duke of Wellington's eye as regards the *meum* and *tuum* in 'cultural valuables,' it was as nothing to the beam in the eye of Napoleon. Once more, acts alleged in the Nuremberg Indictment to have been 'crimes' when performed by Germans were being paralleled by the western victors.

Then there was the charge of 'degradation of the standard of life of the civilian population'. The shortage of food in towns of the Russian zone of occupied Germany, and the difficulties which individual households had in obtaining it, are eloquently described in the German novel published in Switzerland upon which I have already drawn.[2] There have been numerous other sources of information. Weeks went by without any milk being available, except a pint a week for small children. As time elapsed and daily life reached a relative stability,

[1] *Daily Graphic* (London), 13 May 1948.
[2] *Zwischen Braun und Rot*, op. cit.

individual Germans hungered and pined for a morsel of meat. The main articles of diet allowed to them were potatoes and bread. The supply of bread was kept up by having millers mix into the flour other ingredients besides the bread grain. Till the summer of 1947 the supply of potatoes was regular also. But there had been a great loss of potatoes in the preceding winter, and by the summer the loss was making itself felt. Vegetables, and especially fresh vegetables, were a great rarity for towns-people. Store-houses and stores called *gastronoms*, at which they could be bought, were for Russians only. A so-called land reform was held responsible for poor harvests. The land was divided into small holdings, and the holdings were allotted primarily on grounds of political allegiance. Lack of skill and a dearth of implements had lamentable results. Two-thirds of all vegetables grown had to go to Russia, and in the spring of 1947 many smallholders were sent to prison owing to their failure to make the required deliveries of grain and other produce. Russian soldiers would seize a lorryload of vegetables at the very doors of a German hospital or outside a greengrocer's. While food was being kept from Germans in that way every Russian soldier in the zone had to be provided with 28 lb. of meat a month, although later the quantity was reduced. Every Russian child up to the age of eleven was being provided with a quart of full milk and three eggs a day, and there were a lot of Russian children. In July 1947 at Potsdam alone 2,800 children of families of the Russian army of occupation were going to school.

Bad as the 'degradation of the standard of life' might be in the Russian zone, in the French it was worse. There, in the summer of 1946, the ration of the German population was below a thousand calories a head a day, and the inhabitants of the zone were easily the most badly fed in the whole country. At the end of 1947 their food was a little more ample, but every French person had to be provided with 3 lb. of butter and forty-eight eggs a month, and there were a lot of French persons— eighteen for every thousand Germans as compared with two or three Americans to every thousand Germans in the American zone. The Germans in the French zone were getting meanwhile 5¼ oz. of butter a month and forty eggs a year. In one month at the end of 1947 the total meat available—1,403 tons—was divided almost equally between the six million Germans of the zone and the hundred thousand French. That is to say, each French person received as much meat as fifty-five or fifty-six Germans did. Then, too, groups of children from different parts of France were sent to the French zone for periods averaging four weeks. These children were fed on what was indeed the fat of the land, and they were sent home with food in quantity. All this could not last, and for the sake of the production of the zone it was decided in 1947 that food imports would have to be increased fourfold.

In the American zone Germans in towns who went without food for the sake of their children were described by one visitor as 'unimaginably thin'. In November 1947 the economic division of United States military govern- ment in the zone issued a report, according to which in both the British and American zones the production of food was yielding less than a thousand calories a head, and imports of food were considered to provide another 670 calories. In March 1948 in towns of the American zone the fat ration a head a month was 17 grammes, and it takes 100 grammes to equal 3½ oz. In May 1948 a single American CARE parcel contained more meat than a household of five persons in a town of the American zone could obtain in the rations in a month. This was the state of affairs notwithstanding that imports of food into the British and American zones for the year 1948 had been estimated as likely to cost $605 million.

In the British zone in July 1946 the fat ration was

1¾ oz. a week against 7 oz. in England, and the sugar ration 2¼ oz. a week against 8 oz. in England. In mid-July 1946 the potato ration in the zone was honoured for the first time in six weeks. Before the previous occasion on which it was honoured, there had been no potatoes issued since Christmas. Nor did the food supply increase. During the spring and early summer of 1947 the average ration obtainable by a German was about a thousand calories a day, often considerably less. Only in the autumn of 1947 did the ration improve. It was climbing towards, and in some places had reached, the level of 1,550 calories. In 1945 that value of the diet in the zone had seemed shameful. In the month of September 1947 Mr. Victor Gollancz visited Germany with two British members of Parliament, and in describing subsequently what he had seen he stated:[1]

In spite of the improvement, this was the day's diet for each of a family of six in the first bunker-cabin I visited: breakfast—two slices of bread and jam, ersatz coffee, and skim milk; dinner—three small potatoes with vinegar, a cup of skim milk; supper—one and a half herrings, two slices of dry bread, skim milk. The bread was of horrible quality, and there was no butter or margarine. But this was, I think, rather unusually bad, and should not be taken as typical. . . .

I should say that ten per cent., including many of the old, the sick, and the war widows, are starving . . . ; that for twenty-five per cent. the diet is a daily experience of dull and devitalizing misery; that fifty-five per cent. 'get through' on varying degrees of austerity; and that the remaining ten per cent. enjoy anything from reasonable comfort to gross luxury.

The 'degradation' was not only a matter of food. At the end of 1946 the French authorities found that in their zone the empty shops were adversely affecting production and they supplemented imports of food with

[1] *Manchester Guardian*, 11 September 1947.

a diversion to German consumers of the goods produced in the zone. It was arranged that Germans should have a percentage of what they were producing, and that the percentage should be in proportion to the total of production. As regards the British zone, Mr. Gollancz, in a second article, wrote:[1]

I understand that the mysterious Hamburg survey found that 30 per cent. of those examined had no shoes at all or some kind of ruined footwear that was 'quite unweatherproof'. Still, the improvement is considerable. In Schleswig-Holstein, for instance, it is estimated that only 300,000 to 400,000 children will be without reasonable shoes this winter, as against, say, three-quarters of a million last.

He went on to say that in Dortmund, with a population of 450,000, no clothing ration coupons were allocated in May, June, or July 1947 for men's suits, women's underwear, or baby linen, and that in Herford, with a population of 49,000, twenty working jackets and thirty-four working trousers for men, ten slips, ten nightgowns, thirty-four brassières, and fifteen knickers for women, 112 vests, 522 napkins, 386 'muslin napkins', and ten small sheets, for babies, formed the total of clothing made available. No electric light bulbs were being sold to ordinary Germans. Drinking-glasses, plates, wash-basins, and so on, were available at the rate of one a year for every two inhabitants, or one a year for every seven, or one a year for every 150, according to the town. Brooms, brushes, and shaving brushes did not exist. Toothbrushes were for miners only. In Essen there had been no soap for four weeks.

In this second newspaper article, Mr. Gollancz spoke also of housing. He stated that of five and a half million dwelling units in the British zone before the war, 1.6

[1]*Manchester Guardian*, 12 September 1947.

million had been destroyed or irreparably damaged, and another 1.4 million were damaged but reparable. It did not appear that housing repairs were being very swift. In Düsseldorf, in July 1947, there were, he wrote, 3,040 persons without a home and 13,000 living in cellars, bunkers, and the like, against 3,018 and 13,500 on 1 November 1946. He deplored that preparations for establishing a leave centre at Düsseldorf were nevertheless in full swing. The remaining inhabitants had been ordered to leave the neighbourhood so that the centre could be housed, and building materials were to be available for it.

In June 1948 the currency was changed in the British and American zones. Long before that, wages had been falling, prices rising. At the end of 1946 it was estimated that an average German family whose monthly expenditure was 302 marks had to obtain 130 of those marks from savings.[1] In Hamburg in February 1947 the amount of distress might be measured by the arrangements being made to feed 225,000 persons communally and by a rise of five thousand in one week in the number of unemployed. In Berlin at this same time fifteen thousand persons were found to be in need of assistance.

It might of course be argued that the under-nourishment of Germans in the western zones was aggravated, either by neglect or as a result of deliberate policy. But here I am not concerned to discuss whether in fact the 'degradation of the standard of life' of civilians in occupied territories was avoidable either by the victors in Germany or, earlier, by the Germans elsewhere. I am not concerned to discuss whether the Germans, having had the blockade to contend with, could yet have ensured that the inhabitants of the countries which their armies overran were better fed. It is enough for my case that

[1] *Löhne und Preise.* Niedersächsisches Institut für Wirtschaftforschung in Vorbereitung. Clausthal-Zellerfeld, Harz, December 1946.

here is a kind of alleged 'war crime' of which, regardless of circumstances, the vanquished were accused and convicted, and that, whatever the circumstances, the victors are found to have committed it also.

So with other heads under which the vanquished were accused and convicted of 'plunder of public and private property'. It is true that Britain and the United States, far from drawing any profit from their occupation of Germany, were put to heavy expense. It was Russia and France alone that exploited the people and the resources of occupied territory to their advantage, and Russia and France alone that made German industry subservient to their needs. Yet, if the seizure of raw materials and the directing of the resources and production of the occupied country were at first common to the Russians and the French alone, the British and the Americans must be held to have adopted a kindred policy when, in the early summer of 1948, the three western victors agreed that disposal of the production of the Ruhr industrial district should be placed under international economic control. Again, although the 'abrogation of the rights of the occupied people to develop or to manage agricultural and industrial properties' was strictly peculiar to the Russians, who carried out a large-scale 'socialization' of factories and evicted owners of estates and of larger farms without a penny of compensation in order to set up a system of small holdings, the seizure of industrial machinery throughout the country inevitably led to the 'abrogation' of such rights elsewhere.

Between French and Russian policy there was a sharp difference. Whereas the Russian occupation authorities behaved as though Germany were to be given sooner or later the nominal independence of a satellite state, the French occupation authorities looked to the permanent economic union of their area of the occupied country with France itself. Nevertheless all four victors plundered.

Immediately the Russian armies had taken possession of their area of occupation, about three-quarters of the live stock was removed to Russia and much of the remainder was slaughtered so as to provide each Russian with his or her monthly ration of meat.

As for industry, after seventeen months of occupation, the Berlin correspondent of *The Times* wrote as follows:[1]

The picture which emerges is of a part of Germany working almost exclusively in the Russian interest. It is reliably estimated here that, food apart, the Russians are taking from the zone as reparations seventy per cent. of current production, and that of the remaining thirty per cent. a large part goes to the Russian army of occupation. . . .

Three types of control factories are now at work. These are:

(1) Control by headquarters of the Soviet military administration at Karlshorst through German central administration for the zone;

(2) Direct control from Moscow for the benefit of the Red Army in Russia and Germany; and

(3) Control by the recently formed Soviet Industrial Corporation. Factories taken over by this corporation are regarded as Soviet property.

Six months later further details came under my eye. A table of dismantling operations carried out in the Russian zone was compiled from data used by the German provincial governments in the zone. It applied to the situation in November 1946. It showed how German industrial production in the zone had been crippled. All plywood factories had been dismantled, and four out of every five iron foundries and rolling mills. One-tenth of all rubber factories had been damaged during the war, and eight-tenths subsequently dismantled. It is only fair to say that of rayon and plastic plants only thirty-five per cent. had been dismantled, and of shoe factories only

[1] *The Times* (London), 27 September 1946.

fifteen per cent. It was metallurgical and mining plants that had suffered most. Figures for industrial production in Thuringia during October 1946 made it clear that in an average *land* or province of the Russian zone eighty per cent. of such plants had been dismantled and that another thirteen per cent. was under Russian control. The Germans were left with seven per cent.[1] It was usually where factories or else the staff could not be moved that management was transferred to Russian companies.

Another means of obtaining reparations was the placing of Russian orders with German firms for a wide variety of goods. A quantity of these were re-exported by the Russian government. An official black market was conducted in order to obtain scarce goods from other zones.[2]

I have previously quoted from the report made public in November 1947 by the economic division of United States military government in Germany. Let me refer to it again. It stated that if the British and American zones were unproductive, it was not only owing to the drain on production in the Russian zone, where thirty per cent. was taken as reparations, and three-quarters of the foreign trade was with Russia, but also owing to the drain on raw materials in the French zone.

Allowing for differences in outlook and in the standard of life among the Russians and the French, the policy in the area of Germany in French occupation was identical with that in the Russian zone. By the end of 1947 there had been, in the French zone, three separate waves of dismantling factories. As the Russians reduced double line railways to single, so the French in August 1946 were removing one of the two lines of the Freiburg-Mülheim-Offenburg railway. The only difference was in the object. With the French, the object was not the pos-

[1] *Manchester Guardian*, 19 March 1947.
[2] Peter Nettle, 'Inside the Russian Zone, 1945-1947' in *The Political Quarterly*, vol. XIX, No. 3, July-October 1948.

session of metal, but diversion of the important north-south traffic to French railway lines on the left bank of the Rhine. When a plant for the manufacture of surgical instruments was removed as a unit, there could be no pretence that it was machinery for armament. At first the French zone was run, like the Russian, at a profit. Between August 1945 and December 1946, even though the zone was working at only two-fifths of its pre-war capacity, manufactured goods worth $30 million were exported, and raw materials worth $31 million. During the same period food to the value of $45 million was imported. The net profit for sixteen months was therefore about $16 million at a time when Britain was spending $320 million a year on its zone.

But the French exploitation proved too fast and furious. If the goose had not been actually killed, at any rate it was drooping into inanition and the eggs it laid, far from being golden, were not even silver-gilt. As we have seen, at the end of 1946 the Germans in the French zone had to be allowed to buy at least a portion of the goods which they were producing. In addition, imports of food had to be increased fourfold. The result was that for the first three months of 1947 the zone had an adverse foreign trade balance of $7 million.

If the British and the Americans were conducting their respective zones at a loss fabulous by comparison, they could not preen themselves with a sense of superior virtue. The Russians and the French were but doing their moderate best to carry out the policy proclaimed in the agreement made by Britain, the United States, and Russia at Berlin in July 1945. What is known as the Potsdam declaration was frequently alleged to have been concocted in the Kremlin. In fact its inspiration was American. Mr. Morgenthau, in the notorious memorandum which he sent to President Roosevelt in the autumn of 1944, recommended that the whole of North-west

Germany, from the Kiel Canal to the Moselle—almost the whole of the area allotted to British occupation—

should not only be stripped of all presently-existing industries, but so weakened and controlled that it cannot, in a foreseeable future, become an industrial area.

The State Department in Washington succeeded in preventing Mr. Morgenthau's recommendations from being adopted *in toto*, but at the end of 1947 two of them were still elements of policy. One was that the quantity of industrial plants in Germany should be reduced by dismantling so as to ensure a certain low maximum of industrial production, and the other was that the removal of dismantled plants to the territory of the victors should serve as reparations. It is true that in the spring of 1946 General Lucius Clay, military governor of the American zone, temporarily suspended removals of industrial plants from the area of Germany in his control. But by then the business had already gone very far. Towards the end of September 1945 General Eisenhower had announced that five of the largest industrial undertakings were to be dismantled and exported to destinations which he did not name. A month later it was announced that the three large chemical plants of the I. G. Farbenindustrie in the American area and five other industrial establishments would be demolished. Moreover, in March 1946 it was given to be understood in Germany that from the British and American zones together the removal of no fewer than 1,636 plants was contemplated. In the British area, in July 1946, one of the largest shipyards in Hamburg was blown up and twelve thousand tons of steels were destroyed.

Not till October 1947 were German industrialists allowed to know if their properties and livelihood were to be sacrificed or to be spared. The British and United

States governments then issued a list containing the names of 682 factories out of a total of fifty thousand said to be standing in the two zones. Of these 682 factories, 186 were in the American and 496 in the British zone. They were stated to be factories that had been, were being, or would be dismantled. But it was added that the total of 682 did not include plants listed in March 1946 as due for removal on the ground that they were engaged in prohibited industries. It was stated that individual machine tools would go on being removed from factories in the British zone not on the list, and sent to countries which had suffered from German 'aggression'. Machinery for making guns would continue to be destroyed. But no more surface buildings would be destroyed, except specifically military constructions.

The publication of the list met with criticism in Britain as well as in Germany. It was pointed out that the list was served up to the Germans like some sort of unpleasant conjuring trick, that the dismantling would require thousands of German workers over a period of two years when Germany was in desperate need of constructive and productive activity; and, lastly, that the list had no finality. It was pointed out that while a great deal of time and an immense quantity of labour were going to be devoted to carrying out the programme of dismantling, the German railways were being allowed to suffer progressive ruin and that rolling stock and locomotives were not being built in anything like sufficient number.

At the beginning of November 1947 Lord Pakenham, at that time British minister in charge of German affairs, stated, in the course of a speech in the House of Lords, that, of the 682 plants which it was intended to dismantle, 302 were 'war plants'. He could not have seen a letter which Messrs. Victor Gollancz and R. R. Stokes had published in a newspaper only two weeks earlier. They pointed out that the figure of 302 was misleading. 'The geographical distribution is', they said, 'of paramount importance. Of the 682 listed 294 are in Nordrhein-Westfalen, and of these only forty-three are described as war plants'. They further mentioned that among the plants to be dismantled as reparations were some for the manufacture of poison gas and V-weapons. 'Why', they asked, should this equipment be delivered to countries 'which, for all we know, might use it against us in another war?'[1]

It was not only factories and factory-equipment that were being plundered in the guise of 'reparations'. Both in the Indictment of the so-called 'major war criminals' at Nuremberg and in the Judgement of the international military tribunal, there were frequent references to the Hague Rules drawn up in 1907 for the conduct of war on land and subscribed to by many countries including the belligerents. I shall have more to say about these references later. But here I may quote Rule No. 55. It is as follows:

The occupying State shall be regarded only as administrator and usufructuary of public buildings, landed property, forests and agricultural undertakings belonging to the hostile State, and situated in the occupied country. It must safeguard the capital of such properties, and administer them in accordance with the rules of usufruct.

To the extent this rule applies to forests, it is to be noted that on 12 September 1945 there was an announcement that 'the forests of North-West Germany' were to be 'exploited to the limit'. Nor was the 'exploitation' confined to one area of occupation. Although the matter attracted no comment in Britain at the time, it was surely of the utmost gravity. Not only was the capital of the country being destroyed, but there was the prospect of consequences for the climate both of Germany itself and of neighbouring countries.

[1] *Manchester Guardian*, 29 October 1947.

To this two sources,[1] independent of each other, testify. One is a letter from a Swiss expert on nature protection with close knowledge of what was taking place in Germany. He wrote:

The deforestation—that is, the clear-cuttings—in Germany are taking threatening forms. The German climate is assuming steppe features (*Versteppung*). This danger ought to be taken seriously, not only in Germany itself but in all of Europe. It is certain that as a consequence climatic changes will take place in Switzerland.

The second source is *Unasylva*, the forestry journal of the food and agricultural organization of the United Nations, which stated:

Many countries view an excessive depletion of Germany's wood resources with grave anxiety as upsetting the whole economic structure and balance of Europe and as mortgaging the future with a problem it will take at least a hundred years to readjust.

Further, German technical experts were taken to Russia. Others were removed to the United States in order to work for the Navy Department or to engage in other research. The industrial correspondent of a London newspaper wrote:[2]

Ten of Germany's foremost V1 and V2 experts are coming to Britain for secret work developing guiding projectiles at the Ministry of Supply establishment at Westcott, Bucks. . . .

Already twenty-six German scientists are working at the Royal Aircraft Establishment, Farnborough, Hants. . . . Five German turbine experts are working for C. and A. Parsons, Newcastle.

[1]Both quoted in Hans Huth's *Report on the Present Situation of Nature Protection in the American, British and French Occupied Zones of Germany* (June 1948), pp. 15-6.

[2]*Daily Graphic*, 1 November 1946.

There was a hunt for chemical formulae and industrial secrets. On 29 July 1946 Mr. R. R. Stokes told the House of Commons:[1]

As an industrialist, I have found the approach of some of His Majesty's government officials on the question of worming secrets out of Germany utterly and completely repulsive. . . . I feel it to be utterly repugnant that, when an enemy is down and out, the industrialists of this country should invade its soil like a swarm of vultures and pick the remaining flesh from its bones.

Fifteen months later Mr. Stokes, in company with Mr. Gollancz, had more to say on the same subject. They wrote:[2]

Germany has been compelled to disclose her industrial secrets —patent processes, recipes, blue-prints, 'know-hows'. This surrender of a vast intellectual capital must gravely handicap her export trade in a competitve world. Prototype machines have been abstracted under the same procedure. . . . There is a further class known as 'multilaterals'—i.e. particular pieces of equipment removed, on reparations account, in advance of dismantling.

Altogether, it is beyond doubt that at the same time as the four victorious powers in occupation of Germany were accusing and convicting the former German leaders at Nuremberg of 'plunder of public and private property' in occupied territories, they were all proving to be formidable rivals of those leaders in obtaining plunder themselves.

[1]Hansard.
[2]*Manchester Guardian*, 29 October 1947.

THE LAST OF THE SIX kinds of 'war crime' dwelt upon by the international military tribunal was 'destruction of cities, towns, and villages, and devastation not justified by military necessity'. The absence of military necessity was obviously a moot point. For hitherto it had been left to military commanders to decide at the time whether or not any destruction was necessary.

In the Indictment former German leaders were accused, and at the Trial they were convicted, of responsibility for the destruction of 'entire villages'. Was that destruction peculiar to Germans? Soldiers who served in British armoured formations have alleged that, as they advanced into Germany, they burned down some villages by firing tracer bullets into houses. An officer of British military government attached to the United States armies entered German territory near Aachen in the autumn of 1944, and almost the first sight that met his gaze was a village in flames. It had been set on fire by the Americans because, so he was told, American soldiers had been killed or wounded by shots that appeared to come from some of the houses. The villagers had not been consulted regarding military necessity.

Of course the greater part of the destruction perpetrated by the victors in Germany took place before the country was invaded. A commission entirely free to be impartial might not consider that military necessity invariably dictated it. In the summer of 1940 the Pope appealed to all belligerents to refrain from the indiscriminate bombing of innocent civilians. He was not heeded. The reason advanced in Britain and the United States for disregarding the Pope's appeal was that mass, indiscriminate bombing would help to shorten the war. Before the war began it was assumed in Britain—as for instance in the manual of the Royal Air Force—that the offensive power of an air force was to be measured by its capacity for 'direct attack on the enemy's will to war'. If the words meant anything, they meant that in war the offensive from the air should be concentrated against enemy civilians—that is to say, non-combatants —so that they might be demoralized and in their panic lead their government to accept defeat. The theory had prominent advocates—Mitchell and Seversky in the United States, and especially Giulio Douhet. The latter's book, *The Command of the Air*, attracted considerable attention, and in 1943 it appeared in an English translation. Its argument was as follows. Nowadays a nation's fighting power depends on industrial production and civil morale. Let those two sources of energy be destroyed, and at once the fighting power will collapse. Therefore, in order to win a war, it was only necessary to gain command of the air and then to bomb factories and civilians till industrial production became impossible and morale was broken. In 1939 and 1940, the British high command half-heartedly adopted Douhet's doctrine— adopted it, that is to say, too weakly to put it to the test, too strongly not to deprive the land forces of valuable support. The British maintained an 'advanced air striking force' in France, with headquarters at Rheims, many miles away from the British expeditionary force, which had its front along the northern section of the Franco-Belgian frontier. As the war proceeded through the years 1940 to 1944, the Royal Air Force multiplied its strength, and presently it was reinforced by the colossal air power of the United States; and during all this time the two allies continued to keep the bulk of their bombers and fighters independent of the land armies. The bombers were concentrated on 'strategic bombing'.

Yet, as far as prosecuting the war went, the results hardly corresponded with the expenditure of treasure and the courage of the air-crews. Of course there was destruction. At Hamburg 6,200 acres were destroyed, at Berlin 5,400 acres by British and about 1,000 by American attacks, at Düsseldorf 2,003 acres, and at Cologne 1,994 acres. At Dresden, Bremen, Duisburg, Essen, Frankfort, Hanover, Munich, Nuremberg, Mannheim-Ludwigshafen, the operational research section of the Royal Air Force measured between one and two thousand acres of destruction in each. In London only about six hundred acres and at Plymouth four hundred acres were destroyed.[1] And in Germany there was heavy toll of life.

During a massive air raid on Kassel in 1943 incendiaries were dropped in profusion on the wooden houses of the old town. The inhabitants ran out into the narrow streets, but only to find their way barred in one direction by a sheet of flame. They then ran in the other direction, only to meet a like scorching barrier advancing towards them. On all sides fire hemmed them in. In two raids on Dresden on the night of 13 February 1945 it was estimated that twenty-five thousand persons were killed and thirty thousand more injured.

But was the German war effort crippled? Far from it. In the elaborate study prepared and published by the United States Strategic Bombing Survey, it has been contended that before 1943, while the German air force was the more powerful, the only effect of the bombing of German cities and towns was to invite retaliation, and that even after 1943, when the allies had command of the air, this bombing was ineffective. It was only after the British and United States land armies had secured aerodromes on French soil that allied air raids made German war production stagger and pause. Then, and only then, the short distance, and also further improvement in radar, made selective air raids at last possible. It is true that those conclusions of the United States Strategic Bombing Survey have been disputed in large part by Marshal of the Royal Air Force Sir Arthur

[1]Marshal of the R. A. F. Sir Arthur Harris, *Bomber Offensive* (1947), p. 261.

Harris. But he admits that 'it was only in the last year of the war that our bombing really began to affect the whole German war machine'.[1]

That was not surprising. Very likely the targets selected for the early British air raids on Germany were places of value to the German war effort, such as munition factories, railway marshalling yards, and power stations. Nevertheless, bombing at that time was so inaccurate that often the targets were unscathed and instead it was homes that were damaged and persons not at the moment engaged in war work—supposing their employment to be war work—who were maimed and killed. Soon also the German anti-aircraft defence became more formidable. It has been estimated that during June and July 1941 only one in four aircraft reported to have attacked their target in Germany actually got within five miles of it, and where the anti-aircraft barrage was especially strong, as in the Ruhr, only one aircraft in ten. The younger Krupp, interviewed by British, or it may have been American, intelligence after the German surrender, testified to the small damage done to production at Essen. Even when new navigational devices reduced the margin of error, British and American bomber pilots could not be given, it was found, anything smaller than a 'target area' to attack. In time even a 'target area' was considered too precise. As it became possible for British and American aircraft to carry out raids a thousand at a time, the practice of singling out 'military targets' within a German town was abandoned. The town as a whole was made the objective. Instead of being given 'target areas', the raiders were sent forth to carry out 'obliteration bombing'.

What of those recognized rules of warfare on the violation of which the international military tribunal at

[1]*Bomber Offensive*, op. cit., p. 262.

Nuremberg placed so much emphasis? If 'obliteration bombing' did not achieve any decisive military effect, its military necessity might presumably be impugned? It is a rule of war that an airman shall not be attacked while he is descending by parachute or indeed at any time when he is separated from his machine, for, apart from his machine, he is deemed to be disarmed. By analogy, it might be argued that even if civilians are engaged in direct war work while they are in the factory, they are entitled to immunity while at home, for they are then separated from their productive machine and are indeed not contributing to the war effort. But 'obliteration bombing' could not distinguish between workers in factories and workers in their homes.

Both in the Nuremberg Indictment and in the tribunal's Judgement, much was made of the mass executions said to have been carried out by Germans in concentration camps by means of gas chambers. Nobody could read the accounts of such executions without horror. But even if the evidence at the Trial about gas chambers erred only on the side of understatement, it may still be wondered if the executions in them were not more humane than many of the deaths inflicted by 'obliteration bombing'. In face of the havoc done by that bombing, the inclusion among the specific 'war crimes' alleged against the Germans in the Indictment of the item:

Over twenty thousand persons who were killed in the city of Leningrad by the barbarous artillery barrage and the bombings——

was verging on the frivolous. But however formidable the damage and destruction done and however great the suffering and loss of life inflicted by 'obliteration' or 'strategic bombing', nothing achieved by means of any single English or American air raid over Germany could compare with the wholesale murder of non-combatants accomplished by the explosion of an atomic bomb. The two atomic bombs, which were let off over Japan, were credited with having caused no fewer than 280,000 casualties. The agonies of many of the injured were too excruciating for an account of them to be published. Two hundred thousand survivors at Hiroshima were made homeless.

When the former German leaders were being tried at Nuremberg for alleged 'violations of the laws and customs of war', the prosecution denied that the German military commanders could judge military necessity. The prosecution claimed that it was for the victims of the alleged violations to judge. Were the Japanese asked to adjudicate on the military necessity of atomic bombs? Although necessity was alleged, it was established later that those bombs were dropped gratuitously, when victory without them was in sight.

I HAVE NOW DEALT WITH ALL SIX OF THE KINDS of 'war crime' named by the international military tribunal at Nuremberg in its Judgement. The kinds of 'war crime' were, let me recall: (1) Murder, ill-treatment, or deportation to slave labour of civilians of occupied territories; (2) Use of concentration camps to destroy opposition; (3) Murder or ill-treatment of prisoners of war; (4) Killing of hostages; (5) Plunder; and (6) Destruction of cities, towns, and villages, and devastation not justified by military necessity. We have seen how untenable is the supposition that in the framing of the Charter for the tribunal, and for that matter in the framing of the Indictment of so-called 'major war criminals', it was considered impossible that any persons except Germans could have committed, or be committing, acts of any of the kinds in the list. And presumably, my dear Daniel, there will be now little doubt in your mind about the meaning of the Pope when, in a passage of his broadcast on Christmas Eve 1945, he said:

> Any one . . . who exacts the expiation of crime through the just punishment of criminals because of their misdeeds should take good care not to do himself what he denounces in others as misdeeds and crimes.

There was not one of the six kinds of 'war crime' named by the international military tribunal in its Judgement which one or more of the victorious powers, who arrogated to themselves the task of punishing so-called 'war criminals' among the defeated, was not open to being accused of. However, about the first clause of the proclamation which the Control Council of the victors issued to the German people in October 1945, that first clause which affirmed 'All persons are equal before the law', I have not yet said all. There remain the two kinds of 'crime against humanity': (1) Persecution, repression, and murder of political opponents in Germany; and (2) Persecution of Jews.

AS YOU WILL SEE when I come to examine briefly the Judgement of the international military tribunal, the tribunal found Count Four of the Indictment—'crimes against humanity'—a source of some embarrassment. That is not surprising. Nevertheless, the tribunal pronounced a number of the accused whom it declared

118

guilty to have been guilty under this Count, fifteen of them to be exact, not to mention Bormann who was tried *in absentia*. Hence, in view of the Control Council's affirmation that 'All men are equal before the law', it will be pertinent to inquire if the victors also could not have been reproached with each of the two kinds of 'crime against humanity'.

With regard, first, to the 'persecution, repression, and murder of political opponents in Germany', the public of the world was treated on the eve of the German surrender to a wealth of sensational description of the revolting conditions in German concentration camps. Of other, non-German, concentration camps it was told little, either then or afterwards, and of many of them nothing has appeared in the newspapers of the West. An announcement made at Nuremberg in July 1946 during the Trial had a doubtless unconscious yet sardonic humour in it. The announcement was that the American delegation to the peace conference then being held at Paris had under consideration to propose that clauses concerning the curiously named crime of 'genocide'— the attempted extermination of a racial group—should be included in all peace treaties, and that every government signing a treaty should be compelled to include in its criminal code a provision that 'whoever attacks the life, liberty, or property of a national, racial, or religious group, is guilty of genocide'.[1]

What gave this announcement a sardonic humour was that, as regards the 'persecution, repression, and murder of political opponents', or, in other words, the 'crime against humanity' of 'genocide', there were then concentration camps (or their equivalent) for 'national, racial', or political groups in Poland, Czecho-Slovakia, Yugoslavia, Rumania, Bulgaria, Hungary, Belgium, and

[1] *The Times* (London), 30 July 1946.

France, to say nothing of other countries. The offence of the persons confined in those camps was precisely the offence on account of which from 1933 to 1945 Germans were put into concentration camps in Germany. They professed opinions repugnant to the government. As I have said, little or nothing is known of the conditions in such camps. Even if the treatment of the inmates was all that could be desired, those inmates would still be persons deprived of liberty and of the enjoyment of property. Those of them who belonged to racial or political minorities would still be the victims of 'genocide'.

For that matter, the 'persecution and repression' of political opponents is something not altogether unknown in either Britain or the United States. As I write, certain persons in both countries are being penalized either for their professions of political belief or else for the political beliefs of which they are suspected. Imprisonment? In the one country, that has been symbolized by the name of Sir Oswald Mosley; by the name of Eugene Debs in the other. If you were to tell me that Debs was convicted of attempting sedition and that for Sir Oswald Mosley to remain at large during the war would have been contrary to the 'public interest', I would say, in the first place, that no charge was preferred against Sir Oswald Mosley, and that, in any event, the objections were irrelevant. The term 'public interest' is vague and can be used to disguise reasons which neither Parliament nor people is allowed to examine. But however cogent the reasons for the imprisonment of a political offender may be, they cannot weigh here, for no reasons weighed in the Nuremberg Trial. The tribunal held that to persecute and to repress political opponents was wrong, and wrong without qualification. That raised a number of disturbing questions. We are brought to ask, for instance, at what stage do persecution and repression begin to be wrong? Are they wrong in principle, and is it therefore wrong to persecute and repress even a single political opponent? Or have a certain number to suffer before persecution and repression become wrong? Or, again, was it only wrong for German National Socialists to persecute and repress political opponents, and not for others?

If numbers are considered essential, then let it be noticed that the German evacuation of France in 1944 was followed by a French orgy of banditry and of venting personal spites. By mere gratuitous delation your covetous neighbour could gain possession of your house or apartment, or of your business, and thousands of men and women were crowded into prison.[1]

If numbers are considered essential, there is Czecho-Slovakia. In London on 1 February 1945 Dr. Beneš issued a decree for the trial and punishment of alleged 'war criminals, traitors, and collaborators', the term 'war criminal' being restricted to Germans or persons of German or Austrian origin, and the terms 'traitors' and 'collaborators' applying to Czechs and Slovaks. This first decree was amplified by Decrees Nos. 16 and 17 of 9 July 1945 setting up so-called people's courts and courts of honour. The courts were not dissolved till May 1947. They are officially stated to have tried nearly thirty thousand persons in Bohemia and Moravia alone. Prague in the last months had as many as thirty people's courts to itself.

Altogether about eight hundred persons were sentenced to death, another eight hundred to life imprisonment, and 19,888 to various terms of imprisonment up to twenty years. The 19,888 had to serve the first half of their sentence in a concentration camp, and, if they survived that, the second half in prison. Forty thousand persons were arrested and released, but only to be punished by national councils. These were bodies formed

[1]Cf. Sisley Huddleston, *Terreur 1944* (Paris: Editions de la Couronne, 1947).

121

by a show of hands at mass meetings convened for the purpose.

Ill-treatment? In 1947 there were in Czecho-Slovakia fifty-one concentration camps. Mr. R. R. Stokes visited one in September 1946, and in a letter published in an English newspaper[1] he subsequently described what he had seen. He then estimated the diet of each inmate at 750 calories a day. The figure speaks for itself. One morning at six o'clock he saw hirers of labour arrive at the camp by car and lorry and select their slaves for the day. All but the old and a number of so-called 'dangerous persons' were available for hire (without pay), and any one who refused was liable to be beaten. But refusals were rare, for going out had the advantage of ensuring one square meal.

If numbers are considered essential in order for political repression to be wrong, there is Russia. I have already written of the deportations that took place from 1939 to 1945 into the interior of Russia or Siberia from Poland, the Baltic States, Bessarabia, and Northern Bukovina. As I have said, the deportees from all those places were sent to one of three destinations. They went either to so-called 'free exile', to prison, or to lagier. Whichever it might be, Russians were found to be already there. The existence in Russia of lagiers or corrective labour camps has become notorious. Much of what has appeared in print about them in English or in French may be disputable, for the facts are hard to get at. Hints may be derived from a study of the Russian newspapers, but no precise information is issued by the Russian government. We in the West have had to be content with the reports which released Poles and one or two escaped Russians have made of their experiences. However, it is agreed that if the inmates of the camps include some who in Britain or

[1] *Manchester Guardian*, 10 October 1946.

the United States would be put in prison, the majority are political offenders.

It is agreed that, notwithstanding a Bolshevik theory of the redemptive value of hard work, few of these can become 'better men'. It is agreed that confinement in a lagier amounts to 'persecution and repression', and often means murder by degrees. For, as I have said, the conditions in most of them are inhuman. Callousness, indifference, and brutality are the rule. The inmates have to work. Their working day—working, walking, or standing—is normally of fifteen to sixteen hours. They are fed, but only enough to keep them working and not always enough for that. They are paid, but too little to matter, and there is hardly anything for them to buy. They may sleep in holes in the ground. They are clad in rags and tatters. Many of the camps are within the Arctic circle. Others are in swamps or forests. In such camps only the most stalwart can hope to survive for long. And what have they to survive for? If they are at length released, it is only to be retained in the neighbourhood. They have, moreover, been irreparably degraded. 'The most fearful iniquity of the system', according to the anonymous author of *The Dark Side of the Moon*, ' . . . is the corruption, the progressive and irreparable corruption of *everybody* within its spread.' There is, the author says,[1]

The knowledge that, like hell, it is eternal and goes on for ever. That there is no question of holding out within yourself for, say, three years, or even five or eight (in most camps a physical impossibility anyhow) and remaining yourself, or some shadow of yourself, and then leaving it behind. *Nobody leaves lagier behind. Lagier is for ever.*

It is agreed that the Russian 'political offenders' who have been confined in lagiers number millions. The

[1]P. 107, italics in the text.

term 'political offender' has to be taken in a wide sense. As is said in *The Dark Side of the Moon*,[1]

> Confronted with ignorance and apathy, with 'obstruction', 'sabotage' and even physical resistance, the Russian Bolshevik Communist Party found itself committed to more and more military expeditions, more and more 'industrial penetrations', and—increasingly and on a growing scale after the death of Lenin—to more and more liquidations, 'pacifications', mass deportations and 'purges'. . . . They waged a whole series of unpublicized civil wars. . . . They 'pacified' whole Republics, as the Caucasus and the Ukraine. . . . They 'liquidated' the farmers, the nomad societies of the north and east, and the whole Socialist opposition within the Party.

In 1932 thousands of Ukrainians were deported to a single camp in the north-west of Siberia. Twenty were still there in the summer of 1940, eight years later. They are stated to have been the sole survivors. As time passed, persons sent to lagiers included 'offenders against the Soviet way of life' and persons suspected of communicating with foreigners. At the end of the war they included thousands who were suspect of willing or unwilling collaboration with the German invaders.

Furthermore, the Russian government, once in occupation of a vast area of Germany, opened concentration camps there and quickly resorted to the 'persecution and repression' of 'political offenders' of another nation. In 1946 the Russian administration in Germany invited the German Socialist party to amalgamate with the Communists. Many of the Socialists who refused were seized and put behind barbed wire. Two other parties were allowed to subsist. They were the Christian Democrats and a resuscitated Liberal party. But the price of their survival was implicit acceptance of every item of Russian policy, and any member of them who displayed

[1] P. 19.

the least independence shared the fate of recalcitrant Socialists.[1]

As for the second kind of 'crime against humanity' of which the former German leaders were accused at Nuremberg, and a dozen of them convicted—'persecution of Jews'—I am going to say something which at first may sound outrageous. Nevertheless, I am confident that on reflection you will agree with me. What I say is this. The treatment called 'denazification' to which so many Germans were subjected after the unconditional surrender is the equivalent of 'persecution of Jews' by the German National Socialists in the twelve years before. 'Denazification' was the wholesale arrest, internment, proscription, and frequently sentence of former members of the German National Socialist party. It was carried out in part by each of the four occupying powers, in part by the Germans themselves (of course Germans who had not belonged to the party). But that is a distinction without a difference. The occupying powers were ruling Germany. Germans acted only at their bidding and with their acquiescence.

If the number of Jews in Germany who were persecuted under Hitler was very large, so was the number of Germans affected by 'denazification'. In November 1947 Lord Pakenham stated in the House of Lords that although twenty-five thousand of the Germans taken into custody in obedience to the policy of 'denazification' in the British zone had been released within the previous year, sixteen thousand were still awaiting trial. By 3 January 1948, out of a population of twenty-two million in the zone, no fewer than 2,144,022 persons had been

[1]Cf. 'Inside the Russian Zone, 1945-1947', by Peter Nettle, *The Political Quarterly* (London), vol. XIX, No. 3, July-October 1948.

examined. Of these 347,667 had been removed from public office or private position. In the American zone the proceedings seem to have been more swift and to have involved still more persons. By May 1947, 3,330,557 Germans had already been examined there. Of these 251,845 persons had been sentenced and 310,000 had benefited by an amnesty. This did not mean that 'denazification' had ended in the American zone. In May 1948 it was announced[1] that 355,000 cases had been disposed of in the preceding April. Altogether 397,928 Germans had then been fined, 6,861 sentenced to confinement in a labour camp, and 24,000 sentenced to 'special labour'.

It might be objected that all this was incomparable with what happened to Jews in Germany between 1933 and 1945 because German National Socialists were not, as were Jews, put to death as National Socialists. In fact, however, the international military tribunal at Nuremberg, in its Judgement, did not pronounce any of the accused guilty of being responsible for the deaths of German Jews. The Jews who were stated to have been killed were from occupied territories. From Germany under Hitler, most if not all Jews who could afford it were up to the outbreak of war allowed to emigrate. No former National Socialist was allowed after 1945 to leave Germany. Those Jews who remained in Germany under Hitler were, the tribunal stated in its Judgement, declared to be foreigners and 'not permitted to hold office'. 'Restrictions were placed on their family life and their rights of citizenship'. To quote further from the Judgement, 'in the autumn of 1938' there occurred 'the burning and demolishing of synagogues, the looting of Jewish businesses, and the arrest of prominent Jewish business men'. Except for the burning and demolishing of synagogues, all these

[1] *New York Times*, 5 May 1948.

things were paralleled after the German surrender in the treatment meted out to former National Socialists.

The case for 'denazification' was of course so obvious that I hardly need to recall it. The case was that the leaders of the German National Socialist party committed while in power the 'crimes' of which they were convicted at Nuremberg. That is to say, they used their power in order to become 'major war criminals'. They had been put into power thanks to the number of their supporters. Hence to have been a member of the party was to have been an accessary of their crimes. It is indeed indisputable that under National Socialist rule Germany was brought to ignominy, disaster, and ruin. But that was Germany's affair. I would remind you too that the 'persecution of Jews' did not take place without a pretext either. It was alleged that in the years from 1918 to 1933 certain Jews— many of them immigrants from the East—took advantage of the vicissitudes with which Germany was afflicted, that they waxed rich at the expense of the people in general and obtained in the economic life of the nation a preponderance excessive in respect of their number. Thus, the case for 'denazification' had been preceded by a case for persecuting Jews.

Furthermore, the injustice of the persecution of Jews was matched by injustice in the carrying out of 'denazification'. Even if true, the allegation about the behaviour of Jews in Germany from 1918 to 1933 could involve only certain Jews. The repressive measures enacted and carried out against Jews affected more or less all of them. The innocent were made to suffer for the guilty, supposing there were any guilty. So with 'denazification'. Among the millions of Germans who had joined the National Socialist party, many had sincerely expected that the party programme would achieve the salvation of their country. Many became members solely in order to retain their means of livelihood. It could be argued that in addition

the doctrine of National Socialism was in no way to blame
for the dreadful evils which befell the country, but that
these were due to the folly of a handful of leaders who,
while professing to abide by the doctrine, actually wielded
power according to their personal whim. Yet 'denazification' did not invariably operate so as to spare the innocent
and to punish only the guilty, if guilt there were, not
merely misguided patriotism. Indeed, the way in which
'denazification' led to abuses was the subject of protest.
Prominent Lutheran ministers, including Pastor Martin
Niemöller and Dr. Helmut Thielicke, professor of divinity
at Tübingen, granted the victors' premiss that 'denazification' was essential to the future health of Germany. But
they objected vigorously to the glaring injustices that were
committed in its name. Among the objections to the official
repression of political opinions, especially when those
opinions have formerly been in fashion, none have greater
validity than that the door is opened to gratifying personal
rancour, that covetousness is encouraged, and that false
testimony can be a source of profit. 'Denazification' was
also unjust in other ways.

The international military tribunal at Nuremberg
acquitted three of the so-called 'major war criminals' who
had held office under Hitler. They were Dr. Hjalmar
Schacht, the banker and economist; Baron von Papen,
the former chancellor; and Hans Fritzsche, who had been
head of the broadcasting division of the German ministry
of propaganda. After his acquittal, von Papen stayed in
the prison buildings at Nuremberg, afraid to come out.
Dr. Schacht and Hans Fritzsche did go out, but they had
nowhere to go. All three of the acquitted were refused
entry and asylum in the British and French zones. Com-
menting on this, the *Manchester Guardian* said:[1]

[1] 8 October 1946.

If Nuremberg administered justice, this is its mockery. . . . Those whom the Powers have set free should not be subject to further processes, and even to fears of assassination. The present plight of these three men is a disgrace to their great judges, for the writ of the Powers runs through the length and breadth of Germany and they cannot disclaim responsibility for anything that happens there.

Needless to say, such protests went unheeded. The three men set free by the international military tribunal —Dr. Schacht, Baron von Papen, and Hans Fritzsche— were presently re-arrested by the German police, and after some further months in prison each was sentenced by a denazification court to serve eight years in a labour camp.

Long before the Nuremberg Trial ended, a special ministry to deal with denazification had been set up by the provincial government of Bavaria, in the American zone. This department ordered the arrest of the wives of a number of the men in the dock. These wives were interned in a camp near Augsburg.

You may estimate for yourself the worth of some of the charges on the strength of which denazification courts passed sentences when I remind you that on 1 September 1948 Dr. Schacht had his conviction quashed by the appeal court at Ludwigsburg internment camp, and the next day was released.

As with the six kinds of 'war crime' of which the so-called 'major war criminals' were accused and sixteen of them convicted, so with the two kinds of 'crime against humanity'. At the Nuremberg Trial the principle of justice, that 'all men are equal before the law', was altogether contemned. In October 1945 the Control Council for Germany, representing the four victorious powers that instituted and held the Trial, reaffirmed the principle in a proclamation to the German people. In the course of the twelve months that followed, the German people were to be shown unmistakably that the principle did not apply between victors and vanquished. The victors were not to be subject to the law equally with the vanquished. The 'law' was for the vanquished alone. I have already reminded you of what the Pope said in the course of his broadcast on Christmas Eve 1945. Two and a half years later, in June 1948, the words of His Holiness were very properly echoed by Dr. Theophil Wurm, provincial bishop of Württemberg-Baden. The bishop said:[1]

If trials of war criminals are to be conducted on the basis of international law, then crimes which Germans have committed cannot be condemned in the name of justice and silence maintained in the name of the same justice about other crimes and criminals of a similar kind.

BY NOW YOU will agree that for the western victors after the war, and in association with their great ally of the East, to have preferred against individuals among the vanquished the charges on which those individuals were tried and all but three convicted by the international military tribunal at Nuremberg was not the legitimate and righteous proceeding which the public was led to believe. There were four charges. The first was the charge that those individuals had conspired or planned to wage 'aggressive war' and the second that they were responsible for 'crimes against peace'. On the first charge eight of the accused were pronounced guilty, on the second twelve. Those two charges may, in the words of the Tribunal have been 'of the utmost gravity', and funda-

[1] As reported in *Der evangelische Sonntagsbote* (Kassel), 27 June 1948.

mental to the whole prosecution. Nevertheless, they were charges that it was quite impossible to substantiate. The third and fourth charges were in another category. The third charge was of responsibility for so-called 'war crimes' and the fourth of responsibility for so-called 'crimes against humanity'. On each of those two charges sixteen of the accused were pronounced guilty. Unlike the first two charges, which referred to a decision the legitimacy of which must be a matter of opinion, they were charges concerned with matters of fact. Actual deeds, not decisions, were alleged, and there is no doubt, moreover, that many such deeds had been done. But in order to sit in judgement *convincingly*, the victors, it may be thought, required clean hands, and their hands were not clean. Deeds of the kinds alleged had not been done by Germans alone. Sixteen of the former German leaders were pronounced guilty of responsibility for six kinds of 'war crime' and sixteen of two kinds of 'crime against humanity', and acts corresponding to each of those kinds of alleged 'crime' had been committed by or in behalf of the victors. It could not be expected that the Trial would go down in history unchallenged, or escape the contempt of posterity, when it flagrantly failed to observe the principle of elementary justice that 'all men are equal before the law'.

There remains a further fundamental question.

Even supposing it had been possible to substantiate the charge of having conspired or planned to wage 'aggressive war' and the charge of responsibility for 'crimes against peace', and even supposing that only Germans had committed acts of the kinds described as 'war crimes' or as 'crimes against humanity', there would still be the claim, advanced in behalf of the western victors, that the Trial before the international military tribunal at Nuremberg was instituted in order to punish criminal infractions of

131

international law, and that the Trial would furnish a precedent for an extension of the dominion of law over the behaviour of sovereign states. In view of that claim, it would still have to be asked if the holding of the Trial was authorized by any body or law, international or other. For if it was not, far from leading to an extension of the dominion of law, it must have been an abuse of law.

The question is therefore fundamental. The answer to it is to be found by considering the Charter of 8 August 1945, by means of which the tribunal received its 'law', and the tribunal's Judgement, which was delivered on two consecutive days, 30 September and 1 October 1946.

The tribunal, in this Judgement, used the phrases 'illegal in international law' and 'crime in international law', and generally spoke as if international law were a body of statutes enacted by some sovereign legislative power, as if international law were a species of criminal law, and as if all that was required for the enforcement of its provisions was the setting up of such a court as the tribunal itself, which might then be left to pronounce penalties according to its whim. It is vital to understand that, in using those phrases and in speaking in that way, the tribunal was seeking to give the words 'international law' a sense which they will not bear.

The words 'international law' do not designate a mystery that only experts should dare to discuss. Their meaning is one which any decent-minded person can understand very readily for himself. Each independent sovereign state has its own laws, and those laws are enforced because two things are recognized. It is recognized that laws are necessary inside a country, and that their necessity implies their respect. It is also recognized that the state has both the right and the power to make and to enforce laws. But between one independent sovereign state and another the situation is obviously different. There is no super-national authority either to make laws that would be binding on states in their relations with one another in the first place; or, still less, in the second place, to enforce such laws. Yet states cannot avoid dealings with one another, and it is obvious that if those dealings are to be conducted satisfactorily certain rules have to be observed. It follows that in practice certain rules are observed, and those rules have come to be known as international law. Their main source is custom and a sense of decency, and their observance is a matter of convenience and morality. Another source is in definite treaties and agreements which two or more states have found it convenient to conclude together. There are, not only the actual provisions of such treaties and agreements, but also rules and customs for the observance and interpretation of the provisions. Thus a large body of rules, customs, and regulations has grown up, and they are punctiliously applied and observed in courts of law, in international arbitration proceedings, and in all certain peaceful dealings in which states are involved with one another. That is to say, they are applied and observed in the dealings of a citizen of one state with the citizen of another state, of one state with a citizen of another, and of state with state. In accordance with the rules, customs, and regulations, damages may be claimed and awarded, but of course only by agreement. In fact, the whole application and observance of international law—using the term in the sense I have explained—is a matter of mutual consent, the consent of the various states concerned in any particular application or observance. Without that consent, international law simply lapses. In the absence of consent, there is nothing to be done except employ force. For one state, or a coalition of states, to seek to enforce observance of some rule or rules of international law on another state is to discard law and to rely on force. And force is foreign to the international law so far considered. The two essential features of the observance of that law are the absence of force and the presence of consent. I have already quoted Lord Maugham, a former lord chancellor, and in order to make plain the presence of those essential features, it is apposite here to quote him again. He says:[1]

> International law means no more than the rules which independent civilized states have agreed to be binding on them in their mutual relations. The Treaty Law of Nations has been much considered by international lawyers and by far-seeing statesmen. There is in general no 'sanction' for the obligations of a treaty, and no court has jurisdiction (except by express agreement) to declare a default and to award damages and to enforce payment. Nor are treaties drafted and agreed in the same way as private contracts, and their terms are in most cases deliberately expressed in the vaguest possible language.

You will notice that Lord Maugham writes categorically, and there can indeed be nothing hypothetical, ambiguous, or disputable about what he refers to.

But of course the words 'international law' are often used with a further meaning. So far I have spoken of international law as a body of rules regulating international relations between both individuals and states while states are at peace with one another. Yet states do not have only peaceful relations. They sometimes go to war with one another. Centuries ago it was realized that in war also it is fitting that states should observe certain rules. In 1625, the Dutch jurist known as Grotius published his Latin treatise entitled *The Law of War and Peace*. In this treatise he set forth the rules which, as it seemed to him, the numerous independent rulers who then exercised sovereignty in western Europe ought to observe in their dealings with one another. He called the treatise *The Law of War* as well as *and Peace*. That is to say, he laid down rules which he thought should be observed in

[1] *The Truth about the Munich Crisis* (1944), pp. 72-3.

134

war as well as rules which he thought should be observed in peace. He spoke of course solely for himself. But it is obviously desirable that wars should be conducted in accordance with at least some rules, and in fact there never was a war in which some rules were not observed. Unfortunately, in the Napoleonic wars and in the later wars of the nineteenth century, the rules were very loose and laxly interpreted and observed. The wounded, in particular, were allowed to suffer needlessly, and while an officer who became a prisoner might have an enjoyable time, for he could give his parole, the common soldier who was made captive had a lot full of hardship and privation. So it was that towards the end of the nineteenth century, and again in 1907, eminent jurists met at The Hague and drew up a new code of rules, which, they agreed, ought to be observed by the armed forces or by civilians in time of war. The code was new, many of the rules were old. The gain was, however, that the codes represented a distinct advance in humanity, that the rules were now clearly set forth, and that they were embodied in various conventions which a large number of governments ratified, and hence undertook to respect.

These rules and usages of war, like the rules and customs which we considered first, were partly drawn from custom and were partly inspired by a sense of the fitting and humane. But even more, if possible, than observance of the other set of rules—the set of rules for peaceful dealings between states—the observance of these rules of war depended on mutual consent. Indeed, if the rules for peaceful dealings are often invoked and applied in law courts, and hence may be called law in the sense in which we speak of the laws of a particular country, these other rules for the conduct of war were at most moral rules.

That does not mean that a belligerent was allowed

no redress if the rules were violated by the enemy. The conventions drawn up at The Hague in 1907 did not mention violations of the rules, but at that time custom had already established that a belligerent could legitimately and morally take certain measures to secure that the enemy should respect the rules, if the enemy showed evidence of ignoring them. The technical name for a violation of any of the rules is 'war crime'.

As a Christian man who, at the commandment of the magistrate, has worn weapons and served in the wars, you know that Chapter XIV of the British *Manual of Military Law* is entitled 'The Law and Usages of War on Land', and that one of the sections of that chapter is headed 'Means of Securing Legitimate Warfare'. It is in that section that we shall find a definition of 'war crimes'. The manual cannot of course be quoted as a legal authority, but it is acknowledged to be an accurate summary of its subject.

In the section 'Means of Securing Legitimate Warfare' is Paragraph 441, and it reads as follows:

The term 'war crime' is the technical expression for such an act by enemy soldiers and enemy civilians as may be visited by punishment of the offenders. It is usual to employ this term, but it must be emphasized that it is used in the technical military and legal sense only, and not in the moral sense.

The next paragraph, Paragraph 442, contains a list of what acts are meant. It reads:

War crimes may be divided into four different classes:—
  (i) Violation of the recognized rules of warfare by members of the armed forces.
  (ii) Illegitimate hostilities in arms committed by individuals who are not members of the armed forces.
  (iii) Espionage and war treason.
  (iv) Marauding.

136

In Paragraph 443 numerous examples are given to illustrate the fourfold classification, and it is clear from those examples that the intention was to restrict the term 'war crime' to acts performed in the actual field of operations.

Altogether, then, the utmost that appeal to international law could do to justify the international military tribunal at Nuremberg and all the other courts in Germany that tried so-called 'war criminals', would have been to give, not a strictly legal, but a moral authority, derived from custom, for the prosecution and punishment of persons convicted of violation of the recognized rules of warfare or of any other kind of 'war crime' in the field. Moreover, international law gave exactly the same moral authority to the German high command. Any belligerent in a war can claim that he is entitled to punish persons guilty of 'war crimes'.

The question arises, and it is a very important one: *When* is it legitimate to punish persons guilty of 'war crimes'? Also it is obviously requisite, if punishment is to conform to approved international custom, that in the prosecution and conviction of offenders no universally recognized principle of elementary justice shall be flouted.

As I have said, in the British *Manual of Military Law*, the punishment of war crimes is specified as simply one of the means open to a belligerent to secure legitimate warfare on the part of the enemy. The whole subject of war crimes is dealt with in that section of the chapter expounding the law and usages of war on land entitled 'Means of Securing Legitimate Warfare'. It would therefore seem that custom and moral law only authorize the punishment to take place *in the field* and *during hostilities*. The whole section supports this interpretation. Paragraph 439 in the section begins by stating that any of the means specified for securing that the enemy shall conduct warfare legitimately may be resorted to, 'as diplomatic intercourse between the contending states is broken off *during a war*' (italics mine). Paragraph 443, in the pre-1944 edition, spoke of the legitimacy of punishing 'officials or commanders responsible' for issuing orders that lead to the commission of war crimes, and no doubt the term 'officials' might be stretched to include 'members of the government', when, as appears to have happened in Germany during the war, members of the government ordered acts in violation of the recognized rules of war. But Paragraph 453 reads:

> The illegitimate acts may be committed by a government, by its military commanders, or by some person or persons *whom it is obviously impossible to apprehend, try, and punish* (Italics mine).

The application of this latter paragraph is clear from the context. Where illegitimate acts are committed by a government or its military commanders who cannot be apprehended *at the time*, instead of the punishment of the illegitimate acts, reprisals may be carried out for the purpose (Paragraph 452) of making the enemy comply for the rest of the war with the recognized rules of war. Clearly, neither in the Hague Rules nor in military law in general is any warrant to be found for seizing the members of any enemy government *after a war is over* and punishing them for war crimes, nor for seizing enemy commanders and individuals and punishing them.

Since the end of the war some English lawyers have argued that it is proper for a state after a war is over to apprehend members of an enemy government and such other enemy individuals as the state may please, and to try and to punish them for war crimes committed during hostilities, as a means of securing legitimate warfare in future wars. Although this argument has been put forward with all the weight of eminent legal authority,[1] it

[1]Cf., e. g. Brigadier-General J. H. Morgan, K.C., *The Great Assize* (London, 1948).

138

is unlikely to carry conviction. After the American Civil War, some members of the defeated Confederate army were tried and punished by the United States government for acts which they had committed or ordered during hostilities. It could hardly be contended that the object of the proceedings taken against those individuals was to secure legitimate warfare in the future. For it was not expected that the Confederate States would again attempt to secede by force. Presumably, once a war is won, the victor does not expect to be fighting the same enemy within a lapse of time short enough for the memory of any post-war punishment of war crimes to have effect. In 1919 it was not a desire to secure legitimate warfare in 1939 that prompted the insertion in the Treaty of Versailles of a demand that the German government should deliver to the victors alleged 'war criminals'. In 1919 it was not expected that the victors would be at war with Germany again within a lifetime. As for future belligerents other than the late enemy, they are unlikely to be deterred from violating the recognized rules of warfare by the knowledge that war crimes had been punished *after* an earlier war; for they will be expecting to win, and will know that provided they win no accusation of having committed war crimes will be brought against them.

The punishment of war crimes *after a war* is bound to be a one-sided affair. During the actual fighting the odds, it may be said, are equal. Neither side may succeed in apprehending many offenders against the rules of war, but at least one side has as much opportunity of doing so as the other side. Afterwards no victor would dream of surrendering to the vanquished army either members of its own armed forces or civilians on the allegation of the vanquished that such persons were accused of war crimes. Hence the net effect of the post-war punishment at the hands of the victor of individuals among the vanquished for war crimes must be to make it seem as if war crimes

139

were legitimate so long as it was the victor who committed them. For that reason, the punishment of war crimes committed in a war that has ended cannot have any influence on the good behaviour of belligerent forces in a future war. The argument that had Britain, the United States, Russia, and France, been content to prosecute and to punish Germans for war crimes alone, and for nothing else, those victorious powers would have been beyond criticism, is not convincing.

For that matter, on one occasion the international military tribunal at Nuremberg dropped the pretence that only Germans could have violated the recognized rules of warfare between September 1939 and May 1945. In reviewing in its Judgement the accusations brought against each of the men in the dock, it delivered, regarding the guilt of Admiral Karl Doenitz, a pronouncement that betrayed the true character of the whole business of victor prosecuting and convicting individuals among the vanquished once a war has ended.

The tribunal in its Judgement stated that Admiral Doenitz 'is charged with waging unrestricted submarine warfare contrary to the naval protocol of 1936, to which Germany acceded, and which reaffirmed the rules of submarine warfare laid down in the London naval agreement of 1930'. Then, having reviewed the allegations of the prosecution, the tribunal proceeded to make a further statement which demands to be quoted in full. It said:

In view of all the facts proved and in particular of an order of the British Admiralty announced on 8 May 1940, according to which all vessels should be sunk at sight in the Skagerrak, and the answers to interrogatories by Admiral Nimitz stating that unrestricted submarine warfare was carried on in the Pacific Ocean by the United States from the first day that nation entered the war, the sentence on Doenitz is not assessed on the ground of his breaches of the international law of submarine warfare.

140

This statement has already attracted comment among Germans, and that is not surprising. It is a curious statement. It is the statement that in one instance no wrong was done when Germans ordered or committed violations of the rules of war because war crimes of the same kind had been ordered and committed by the British and United States high command.

> Thieves for their robbery have authority
> When judges steal themselves.

Regarding the pronouncement, you may wonder, in the first place, why the tribunal confined itself to that single instance. Why did the ordering or commission of other war crimes by the victors not exonerate others of the vanquished? On that point the tribunal, in its Judgement, threw no light.

In the second place, you will notice that in exonerating Admiral Doenitz of guilt for the 'breaches of the international law of submarine warfare' held to have been proved against him, the tribunal did more than declare that in that instance it was legitimate for a German commander to order or to commit war crimes provided similar war crimes had been ordered and committed by British and American commanders. The tribunal further implied that *it was legitimate* for British and American commanders to have ordered whatever violations of the recognized rules of warfare *they chose*, but *not legitimate* for German commanders to have exercised *the same choice*. In other words, according to the tribunal in this portion of its Judgement, not only was a war crime never a war crime unless it had been ordered or committed by Germans; it was not even then a war crime unless Germans had chosen to order or to commit it and the British and Americans had not. That is to say, the tribunal implied that the guilt of which it convicted Germans in regard to war crimes was not guilt of the crimes themselves, but

141

guilt of having presumed *to choose*, in the absence of a precedent on the part of the victors, which crimes were expedient. That choice of the expediency of a crime the tribunal made into a preserve of the victors. Only they were entitled to exercise it.

In any event, it would be thought obviously incumbent upon courts that tried persons accused of disregarding rules which had the approval of a consensus of civilized countries not themselves to violate any principle of elementary justice universally recognized by the same civilized countries. On the contrary, in the trials more than one such principle was violated.

The international military tribunal was appointed by means of an agreement drawn up on 8 August 1945 in behalf of the four victorious powers participating in the institution of the Trial—the United States, Britain, Russia, and France. To this agreement was annexed a Charter which defined the constitution, jurisdiction, and functions of the tribunal.

In this Charter, it was laid down that the tribunal would not be bound by the rules of evidence. In effect, the provision enabled the prosecution to submit to the tribunal during the Trial testimony in the form of affidavits instead of having invariably to produce actual witnesses. At the same time the defence was prevented from obtaining certain testimony, from challenging other testimony, and from examining—in court or elsewhere—the authors of the affidavits. Moreover, the defence suffered other disadvantages. The prosecution had access to a vast reservoir of witnesses in political custody. It had the benefit of the postal censorship then in operation. German defence counsel had to make the best they could, at short notice, of an unfamiliar procedure. They were also handicapped by the sequestration by the victorious powers of the property of the accused and of their wives and children.

In the Charter, at Article 8, it was provided that 'the fact that the defendant acted pursuant to an order of his government or superior shall not free him from responsibility'. That is to say, Germans termed 'war criminals' were denied what is known as 'the defence of superior orders'. I shall come later to the essential portions of the Judgement delivered by the tribunal. But here I may mention that the tribunal in its Judgement stated that the provisions of Article 8 of the Charter 'are in conformity with the law of all nations'. That was a strange statement. For, on the contrary, 'the defence of superior orders' had long been admitted into the law of nations. Rule No. 3 of the Hague Rules annexed to the fourth Hague convention of 1907, for instance, is the declaration that a state shall be responsible for the conduct of its armed forces and officials. As recently as 1936, the British *Manual of Military Law* contained, with regard to war crimes, the following paragraph:

443 (of Chap. XIV). . . . It is important, however, to note that members of the armed forces who commit such violations of the recognized rules of warfare as are ordered by their government, or by their commander, are not war criminals and cannot therefore be punished by the enemy. He may punish the officials or commanders responsible for such orders, if they fall into his hands, but otherwise he may only resort to the other means of obtaining redress which are dealt with in this chapter.

The same rule was contained in the corresponding American basic field manual. (Cf. Appendix, A, p. 179.) Till recently it was a rule universally recognized. After all, it is only common sense that a man is being punished unjustly if he is punished for obeying an order which it was practically impossible for him to dispute.

That was still universally admitted at the time of the Treaty of Versailles. In addition to the 'war guilt' article, there was in that treaty Article 228. This required the

German government to deliver to the victorious allies German citizens termed 'war criminals' of whom a list had been compiled. The German government, needless to say, had not consented to the inclusion of this article in the treaty any more than it had consented to the inclusion of Article 231 (the 'war guilt' article). It met the demand with a protest. It declared that to hand over German citizens to the tribunals of foreign countries would be an abdication of sovereignty, and that German sovereignty required that any so-called 'war criminals' who were Germans should be tried in a German court. It proceeded to enact a special law to make this possible. In 1919 the victorious allies accepted the German proposal, and delivered to the German government a list containing the names of 901 persons. Those of the accused persons in this list who could be traced were tried before the supreme court of Leipzig. Only thirteen were found guilty and sentenced.

Propaganda for the prosecution and punishment after the second war of Germans called 'war criminals' made the most of the small number of sentences passed at Leipzig, but the truth is that if the remainder of the persons tried there were acquitted, it was because they pleaded 'the defence of superior orders', and the defence was accepted.

In 1945 no similar scruples were to prevail. There was among the victors the obvious determination to have as many Germans as possible convicted. The evidence of that determination is a happening in England in 1944. For Article 8 of the Charter, according to which the 'defence of superior orders' would not be entertained at any trial of so-called 'war criminals' held by the victors, there had been 'created' in England a precedent. The precedent had been 'created' sixteen months earlier. In April 1944—that is to say, at a time when the war crimes commission was already hard at work compiling its lists—the War Office in London altered the wording of Paragraph 443 of Chapter XIV of the British *Manual of Military Law*. The recognition of the validity of a plea of superior orders as a defence disappeared. In its place there was inserted an assertion taken from an article being contributed to the *British Year Book of International Law for 1944* by Dr. Hersch Lauterpacht, a former Austrian who had become professor of international law in the university of Cambridge. Paragraph 443 was made to read as follows:

The clearly illegal nature of the order—illegal by reference to generally acknowledged principles of international law so identified with cogent dictates of humanity as to be obvious to any person of ordinary understanding—renders the fact of superior orders irrelevant.

I may remark that the *Year Book* had not been published when the *Manual* was altered, and the War Office must have been supplied with an advance copy of the text, so that the alteration might be made in good time for the hunting down of so-called 'war criminals'. Of the substitution it is enough to say that the new wording took no account of military custom. (Cf. Appendix, B, p. 179.)

You and I, my dear Daniel, have served in only one army. We have served in the British army. We know that in the British army during the war the rule was that if an order seemed wrong to the officer or soldier receiving it, he was to carry it out first and to protest afterwards. Or he could refuse to carry out an order and subsequently argue its legality before a court martial. As prisoners of war in Germany, you and I were also able to observe the rule in another army. In that army—the German army—no order given could be illegal, and no order was ever to be questioned. The custom of implicit obedience was regarded as the firm foundation of the German army's discipline. Hence the alteration in the British *Manual* might have been designed to ensure that any so-called 'war criminals' who had been German soldiers would be punished if a court pronounced them to have been guilty, even though they might have acted only as they had been brought up and taught to act. For in the Charter, the refusal inserted in the *Manual* to entertain 'the defence of superior orders' was repeated.

One consequence was that for some alleged offences—it might be said for most—more than one so-called 'war criminal' was convicted and sentenced. For instance, at Dachau in 1947 the architect of a firm of building contractors was put on trial before an American court and sentenced to twenty years' imprisonment. The ground of his conviction was that the firm had employed labour from a concentration camp. He was not allowed to plead that he had only obeyed orders. At Nuremberg the international military tribunal had sentenced Fritz Sauckel, as 'plenipotentiary general for the utilization of labour', to death, and Albert Speer, as minister for armaments and war production, to twenty years' imprisonment. All the offences of which Sauckel and Speer were pronounced responsible, and for which they were sentenced, included that for which the architect was sentenced at Dachau. Moreover, in other trials other officials intermediate between Sauckel and Speer at the top and the architect at the bottom were tried, and being forbidden to plead 'the defence of superior orders', were sentenced too. The offences or alleged offences of which they were pronounced guilty must likewise have included that for which the architect suffered at Dachau. I say nothing of the character of the charge brought against the latter, except that it gave rise to an appeal against the conviction. My point is only that the refusal to entertain 'the defence of superior orders' inevitably precluded the prosecutors and judges of so-called 'war criminals' in Germany from fixing the responsibility for an act on one person only.

146

One of the kinds of 'war crime' alleged against the accused in the Indictment presented to the Nuremberg tribunal was the killing of hostages. The tribunal in its Judgement pronounced the accusation to have been established, and it laid special emphasis on that particular offence. At one place, having enumerated three kinds of acts, including the killing of hostages, which, it was provided in the Charter, 'shall be a war crime,' the tribunal went on to state that 'in the main these provisions are merely declaratory of the existing laws of war as expressed by the Hague Convention, Article 46'. 'In the main', was good. For, as it happens, nowhere in the Hague Rules is there any reference to hostages. Hostages are not mentioned. It is true that the taking and killing of hostages are practices that have been vigorously denounced by legal writers in this century, notably by the first earl of Birkenhead in his handbook entitled *International Law*. But an individual's condemnation of practices, however vigorous it may be, does not make those practices contrary to the laws and usages of war.

In the Hague Rules themselves various exceptions to their observance are explicitly recognized. Regarding Rule No. 50, which forbids the infliction of collective punishment on the inhabitants of occupied territory, it is to be noted that the British *Manual of Military Law* contains (Para. 458 of Chapter XIV) the remark that 'it may be necessary to resort to reprisals against a locality or community, for some act committed by its inhabitants or members who cannot be identified'. Nothing had been laid down anywhere against the taking and killing of hostages as one among such reprisals.

In many countries occupied by the German armies during the war there arose resistance movements. They were no doubt inspired by a noble purpose. The men and women in those movements wished to free their soil from the heel of the invader. But the warfare which they

147

waged was not invariably in accordance with the rules and usages of war or with the strict observance of treaties. In France, for instance, the activities of the resistance were in flagrant violation of the terms of an armistice concluded with the German government by the legal French government at the latter's own request. In any event, although members of a resistance may have displayed exceptional courage and daring, they were compelled by the nature of their movement to operate by cunning and stealth. The war they waged was a stab-in-the-back affair.

Hence it was with justification, you may feel, that Field-Marshal von Rundstedt, when in the witness-box at Nuremberg on 12 August 1946, declared that he would like to see resistance activities forbidden in future by international agreement.[1]

But, whatever may be thought of those activities, it is beyond question that the first duty of the commander of an army in occupation of enemy country is the protection of his men. If those men are being ambushed or attacked while alone or in small parties, and the assailants cannot be identified, it is only to be expected that he will take and kill hostages as a reprisal, and the legitimacy of reprisals during hostilities in order to deter and coerce has never been disputed. Certain kinds of reprisal have of course given rise to protest, but the principle of reprisals in general has been universally accepted.

In agreeing that the killing of hostages was a 'war crime', the tribunal may be said to have very particularly invited the grumble of Kipling's Saxon, 'This isn't fair dealing'.

[1] *The Times* (London), 13 August 1946.

However, as there was unquestionably a recognized custom of punishing in the field persons guilty of war crimes, and the punishment of such persons by the opposing army in a war had the moral authority of the law of nations, let it be assumed, by impossibility, that for the victors in the war of 1939–45 to prosecute and to punish Germans termed 'war criminals' *after the war had ended* for war crimes committed during the war, was legitimate, even though after the war had ended no prosecutions by German commanders or by a German government were allowed. Let it be assumed, by impossibility, that it really was war crimes that were being condemned, and not, as the tribunal's Judgement regarding Admiral Doenitz seemed to indicate, the crime of having presumed *to choose* which war crimes were expedient. Let it be assumed, by impossibility, that no principle of elementary justice was disregarded, such as the principle that 'superior orders' constitute a valid defence, and that practices such as the killing of hostages, although nowhere defined as contrary to the recognized rules of warfare, could be a ground of conviction. Let all that be assumed, and it would remain that three of the kinds of 'crime' specified in the Charter were 'crimes' hitherto unknown to law, and yet that the tribunal sent men to their death or to imprisonment for having been guilty of them. The three kinds of 'crime' were of course 'planning and waging of aggressive war', 'crimes against peace', and 'crimes against humanity'.

To say that these were 'crimes' hitherto unknown to law means that the acts alleged could not have been 'crimes' at the time they were said to have been committed.

Furthermore, in the provisions of Article 9 of the Charter, the tribunal was empowered to declare a 'group or organization' to have been a 'criminal organization', and at the instigation of the prosecution, the tribunal did pronounce four associations of the former German National Socialist party to have been 'criminal organizations'. But they could not have been 'criminal' at the time they existed.

This brings me to the essential portions of the tribunal's Judgement.

The tribunal began in its Judgement by making two indisputable statements. First, it stated that its jurisdiction was defined in the agreement and Charter of 8 August 1945. Secondly, it stated: 'The making of the Charter was the exercise of sovereign legislative power by the countries to which the German Reich unconditionally surrendered.' The two statements, so far as they went, were straightforward. But as regards the 'crimes' of 'planning and waging aggressive war', 'crimes against peace', and 'crimes against humanity', the promulgation of the Charter was a piece of legislation that differed radically from most other legislation of the Control Council of Germany. Most of the laws which that council decreed were to ensure the *current* administration of a country deprived, at the insistence of the victors, of a government of its own. As regards these so-called 'crimes' the Charter purported to make law *for the past*. Likewise, when the tribunal pronounced certain associations to be 'criminal', it was making law *for the past*.

That was something to which Dr. Stahmer, leading counsel for the defence, could not fail to object. In his opening speech he reminded the tribunal of the adage *Nullem crimen sine lege, nulla poena sine lege*. A person was not to be sentenced to punishment unless he had infringed a law in force at the time of his alleged offence, and that law prescribed a penalty. Dr. Stahmer said that in National Socialist Germany, no doubt, the principle had been set aside, at least partially. But the Control Council set up by the victorious powers for the administration of the country had recently restored it to a place among the rules that were to govern legal procedure for Germans. It was in the teeth of that action by the Control Council that the principle was now being disregarded in the Trial.

The objection was one which the tribunal evidently did not feel it should ignore. In its Judgement it made the following statement:

It is to be observed that the maxim *nullum crimen sine lege* is not a limitation of sovereignty, but is in general a principle of justice.

The statement was at least frank. It was the statement that the four victorious powers, in drawing up and promulgating the Charter, had not been actuated by considerations of justice. Of course there was no limitation on the sovereign power of the victors over the vanquished. They could do whatever they liked. But had it not been bruited abroad that the Trial of the former German leaders, and also all the prosecutions of Germans called 'war criminals', of Germans who had been members of allegedly 'criminal organizations', of Germans styled 'organizers' and 'accomplices', were being undertaken for the sake of justice?

More than six weeks before the war ended, the archbishop of York had stood in the House of Lords and said:[1]

It is for the sake of justice, for the vindication of that underlying sense of the difference between right and wrong, which makes us demand that these criminals should receive their punishment.

What became of that demand, what was the point of talking about 'the vindication of that underlying sense of the difference between right and wrong', if a fundamental principle of justice was to be ignored?

[1]Hansard, 20 March 1945.

Apologists for the Trial, and for the punishment of so-called 'war criminals' in general, had contended, and were to go on contending, that the holding of the Trial would lead to an extension of the dominion of law. But how could the dominion of law be extended by means of the flouting of a fundamental principle of justice?

Furthermore, the tribunal in its Judgement was presently to go on to claim that it was administering 'international law'. How could that claim be true if there was an utter disregard of the adage *Nullum crimen sine lege?*

In the Statute of the Hague permanent court of justice for international arbitration, it had been plainly declared that 'the general principles of law recognized by civilized nations' are a part of international law. The words of that Statute are repeated in the Statute—annexed to the United Nations charter of 1945—of the international court of justice, which has succeeded the Hague court. Among such principles none is more certain than the principle that nobody may be punished lawfully for an act which was not a legal offence at the time it was committed. Till lately every civilized nation had included the principle in its own laws. The Constitution of the United States, in its first article (Section 9, clause 3), prohibits the federal enactment of *ex post facto* law, and a further article (Article 10) extends the prohibition to the individual States of the Union. The principle had been affirmed in all European criminal codes. In the French Penal Code, for example, it is stated at Article 4 that no offence, no misdemeanour, and no crime can be the reason for an infliction of penalties unless there was in existence at the time the offence, the misdemeanour, or the crime was committed a law to forbid it and the law specified the penalties which the agent convicted of infringing the law should incur.

Inasmuch as in the Charter certain acts alleged to have been committed before its promulgation were made crimes provided they had been performed by Germans, clearly the promulgation of the Charter violated the principle. Inasmuch as Law No. 10 of the Control Council of Germany, promulgated on 20 December 1945, provided that 'membership in categories of a criminal group or organization declared criminal by the international military tribunal' 'is recognized as a crime', clearly the promulgation of the law violated the principle. Inasmuch as the tribunal, while claiming to administer international law, complied with the Charter, as it was bound to do, the tribunal clearly violated the principle.

Having declared that 'the maxim *nullum crimen sine lege* is not a limitation of sovereignty', the tribunal went on, in its Judgement, to argue that the principle could be disregarded on the occasion, as the accused must have known that they were doing wrong. Yet it is obvious that to make such an exception is to destroy the rule itself.

I invite you to note, furthermore, that at the time the acts made into crimes by the promulgation of the Charter could have been committed, none of the persons alleged to have been guilty of one or more of them was living in a state of lawlessness. Each was the citizen of a sovereign state that was endowed with an elaborate and complex system of criminal and civil law. Another elementary principle of right, which as such must be part of international law, is that no human being is ever under more than one set of laws at a time. Life would be impossible if it were not so. For this reason, as Professor G. W. Keeton recently pointed out, no English court can accept to apply a rule of international law that conflicts with a British statute or that conflicts with an accepted principle of English common law. Had it really been desired to carry out the prosecution and punishment of Germans according to decency and right, surely their position under German law at the time the offences of which they were accused were alleged to have been committed would at least have been looked into. But neither in the Charter, the Indictment, nor the tribunal's Judgement, was anything said about it.

The struggles or contortions of the tribunal in its Judgement to justify the victors in having made laws *for the past* by means of the Charter were limited. The tribunal said nothing to justify the invention of the novelty termed 'crimes against humanity', although the offences referred to by that name were, however dastardly, clearly unknown to law at the time they could have been committed. The tribunal said nothing to justify the power conferred on it in Article 9 of the Charter to declare a 'group or organization' to have been a 'criminal organization', although no group or association which the tribunal did pronounce to have been 'criminal' could have been 'criminal' before its dissolution at the end of the war. The struggles or contortions of the tribunal in its Judgement to justify the making of retroactive law were confined to a pronouncement on the provision in Article 6 of the Charter that 'crimes against peace' 'are crimes within the jurisdiction of the tribunal'.

Having stated that, in its view, the maxim *Nullum crimen sine lege* 'has no application to the present facts', the tribunal in its Judgement went on to state that this view was strongly reinforced 'by a consideration of the state of international law in 1939, so far as aggressive war is concerned'. The tribunal then stated that at the outbreak of war in 1939 Germany was bound by the General Treaty for the Renunciation of War of 27 August 1928, 'more generally known as the Pact of Paris or the Briand-Kellogg Pact'.

Supposing, for the sake of argument, that that were true, the question would remain why individuals were being put on trial on the ground that the Pact of Paris had been violated. Dr. Stahmer, leading German counsel for the defence, had pointed out in his opening speech that it had never been suggested either in the Assembly or the Council of the League of Nations, nor provided in the Pact of Paris, that individuals should be incriminated on the score that a war had been wrongly begun. Still less had it been suggested to the League, he said, that individuals should be put on trial and, if they were then pronounced guilty, have sentence passed upon them. Regarding this plea, the tribunal, in its Judgement, admitted that the Pact of Paris 'does not expressly enact that such acts [as "aggressive war"] are crimes, or set up courts to try those who make such wars'. But it dismissed the plea, declaring that 'for many years past military tribunals have tried and punished individuals guilty of violating the rules of land warfare laid down' by the Hague convention of 1907, and yet the convention 'nowhere designates such practices as criminal, nor is any sentence prescribed, nor is any mention made of a court'. Thereupon the tribunal declared that, in its opinion, 'those who wage aggressive war are doing that which is equally illegal'.

Dr. Stahmer had also referred to the omission of any condemnation of aggressive war in the United Nations charter. This the tribunal significantly ignored.

Dr. Stahmer had contended that international law is concerned with the actions of sovereign states and does not provide for the punishment of individuals. To this contention the tribunal retorted by declaring that many authorities and instances could be cited 'to show that individuals can be punished for violations of international law.' It then went on to cite one instance: the late Chief Justice Stone on the legitimacy of a state's punishment of spies seized upon its territory.

Here, unquestionably, the tribunal in its Judgement, was being equivocal.

For, in the first place, while it is true that the prosecution and punishment of individuals under international

155

law had of course been common, it is essential to understand what individuals and in what circumstances. Individuals had been punished either by armies in the
field or by civil courts. I have already spoken of the
practice of armies in the field of punishing enemy individuals who were found guilty of violating the recognized
rules of warfare; that is to say, of war crimes. As for
punishment or penalty in a civil court, whenever a state
has happened to prosecute a non-resident foreigner in
one of its own courts, and he has been punished or
penalized, that foreigner has suffered under a rule which
the state of which he is a citizen has tacitly or expressly
accepted. Lawrence, a recognized current authority,
makes that point perfectly clear. He says:[1]

> The neutral individual whose contraband cargo is confiscated
> [by a prize court] suffers under a rule to which his government
> has given express or tacit consent, and if any other rule is
> applied his state will at once protest and demand compensation
> for the injury done to her subject.

Both the rule and the practice are, then, that no individual may be subjected to a judicial process at the
hands of some foreign power in whose territories he does
not reside without the consent of his own state. That may
be said of the punishment of war crimes in the field as
of proceedings in a civil court. For to the practice of
punishing war crimes in the field most states have consented in admitting, even if not also in adopting, it.
Dr. Stahmer was right. No agreement had been made,
and hence no consent, tacit or express, had been given, to
the prosecution of members of the former government of
one nation by governments of other nations.

Moreover, in drawing an analogy between the absence
of any mention of courts in the [fourth] Hague conven-

[1]T. J. Lawrence, *The Principles of International Law* (7th ed., 1937),
Part I, chap. I, section 3.

tion of 1907 and the absence of any mention of a court in the Pact of Paris, the tribunal was not very happily inspired. At the time the Hague conventions of 1907 were drafted, signed, and ratified, the practice of punishing enemy individuals who had been guilty of war crimes and who could be seized was already well and long established. Any mention of courts, supposing punishment had been the object of the conventions, was accordingly superfluous. At the time, however, of the signature of the Pact of Paris no courts for the trial of individuals alleged to be responsible for the violation of an international agreement of its kind had ever been envisaged. Furthermore, there was another reason why the Hague conventions contain no mention of courts. Not one of them was agreed to with the object of ensuring that infractions would be punished. All were drawn up as a means of securing international agreement and observance. The drawing up of the Pact of Paris, it is safe to say, was undertaken with the same moral object. No court was mentioned because neither coercion nor punishment was intended.

In any event, was it true, as the tribunal alleged, that Germany was bound in 1939 by the Pact of Paris? Was it true that, in virtue of the signature of the Pact of Paris in 1928 by a previous German government, the German government of 1939 was barred from resorting to a war if it believed that war to be in defence of the interests of its country? One answer to the question is of course in the words of Lord Maugham which I quoted earlier:

There is a weighty implication to be borne in mind in construing treaties between nations, namely, that according to good sense and to the practice of civilized nations the obligations they contain are regarded as subject to the implied condition that the circumstances under which they were made have not materially changed. In other words, the condition *rebus sic stantibus* is held to apply.

157

And there is a second answer. Having stated that at the outbreak of war in 1939 Germany was bound by the Pact of Paris, the tribunal in its Judgment proceeded as follows:

> The question is, what was the legal effect of this Pact? The nations who signed the Pact or adhered to it unconditionally condemned recourse to war for the future as an instrument of policy, and expressly renounced it. After the signing of the Pact, any nation resorting to war as an instrument of national policy breaks the Pact. In the opinion of the tribunal, the solemn renunciation of war as an instrument of national policy necessarily involves the proposition that such a war is illegal in international law; and that those who plan and wage such a war, with its inevitable and terrible consequences, are committing a crime in so doing. War for the solution of international controversies undertaken as an instrument of national policy certainly includes a war of aggression, and such a war is therefore outlawed by the Pact.

This passage was bound to prove fatal, sooner or later, to the pretensions of the tribunal to have administered international law.

As regards the Pact of Paris, the statement: 'The nations who . . . adhered to it unconditionally condemned recourse to war for the future', contained on the part of the tribunal an ambiguity such as it is the boast of judicial experts that they eschew. Did the tribunal mean that adhesion to the pact was unconditional or did it mean that the condemnation of recourse to war was? In fact, there had been nothing unconditional about either.

In signing the Pact of Paris in 1928, each of the great powers expressly put on record reservations. The British government, for example, reserved its freedom to make war as regards 'certain regions of the world the welfare and integrity of which constitute a special and vital interest for our peace and safety'. The United States expressly reserved its freedom to make war in obedience to the terms of the Monroe Doctrine. As you are not an American, I may remind you that that is the name given to the policy of the United States that President Monroe foreshadowed in 1823, when he declared that the United States would oppose any interference by European states in either North or South America. The French government expressly reserved its freedom to make war in self-defence or in fulfillment of treaty obligations. The other signatories expressed similar reservations. That those reservations had been expressed the tribunal did not mention.

The tribunal's silence on this point was eloquently understandable. That there had been the reservations constituted a fatal objection to the opinion which the tribunal was delivering; namely, that the Pact of Paris had made war 'illegal in international law' and the planning and waging of war 'as an instrument of national policy' into a 'crime'. As no wars are waged except as 'an instrument of national policy', the second part of the opinion was invalidated by the invalidation of the first part. Far from having been a statute of international legislative effect, the Pact of Paris was not even a genuine agreement to refrain from going to war. Under the Pact, war was not to be resorted to only if no 'special and vital interests', no reserved continents, no treaty obligations were involved.

The omission of the tribunal in its Judgement to refer to the reservations which had accompanied the signing of the Pact, and which went far to reduce that document to a pious expression of good intentions, was by no means the tribunal's only piece of tergiversation. It was very free with the word 'aggression', but it nowhere so much as attempted to justify its use of a word, which, as I have pointed out, is really meaningless. Any general agreement on the application of the word 'aggression' in any particular instance has been quite impossible to arrive at.

And it cannot be said that the tribunal, in its Judgement, invariably used the word with care or with regard to all the facts. For example, the tribunal stated that 'the invasion of Austria [in 1938] was a premeditated aggressive step in furthering the plan to wage aggressive war against other countries'. In making that statement, the tribunal was overlooking certain facts. Had it recalled them, it is difficult to see how it could have described 'the invasion of Austria' as an 'aggressive step'. Not only did all four of the victorious powers that sat in judgement on the former leaders of the vanquished in 1945 and 1946 acquiesce in the invasion and annexation of Austria at the time in 1938, but also the annexation had been a step which representatives of at least one of those victorious powers strongly recommended beforehand.

At the trial in Vienna in November 1947 of Mr. Guido Schmidt, last Austrian foreign minister before the incorporation of Austria in Greater Germany (a trial which ended in an acquittal), it was stated in behalf of the defence that when Sir Austen Chamberlain visited Vienna in April 1936, he advised 'that the independence of Austria should be put under the protection of the Reich, and if necessary a sacrifice should be made in home politics'. Evidence was given at the trial that in 1937 Sir Nevile Henderson, British ambassador in Berlin, said to the Austrian minister in Berlin: 'You are Germans. The Germans should be together.' Later in that year Henderson said to Schmidt: 'I don't understand what you want. You are Germans, aren't you?' At the trial the late Lord Salisbury was quoted as having said to an Austrian diplomatist: 'What do you want alone? Why don't you make the *Anschluss*?'[1] The tribunal at Nuremberg neglected to recall in its Judgement how spokesmen of one of the victorious powers, at whose

[1] All quotations from report of the trial in *Manchester Guardian*, 28 November 1947.

instigation and in whose behalf the Trial was being held, had recommended the incorporation of Austria in Greater Germany. Again the tribunal's silence was understandable. For if those recommendations had been recalled, the tribunal would have had to explain how it was that to comply with the recommendation could have been 'an aggressive step'.

I may now sum up the answer to the question: Was the Trial before the international military tribunal at Nuremberg authorized by any law, whether international or other? In the Charter, which defined the constitution, jurisdiction, and functions of the international military tribunal, there were specified three kinds of alleged 'crime' hitherto unknown to law. These were 'planning and waging of aggressive war', 'crimes against peace', and 'crimes against humanity'. In Article 9 of the Charter the tribunal was empowered to declare a dissolved 'group or organization' to have been a 'criminal organization', and the tribunal did pronounce four German associations, off-shoots of a political party, to have been 'criminal'. Accordingly, both in the Charter and in the tribunal's Judgement law was made *for the past*.

That is to say, a cardinal principle of justice and law was disregarded. The principle is that nobody may be punished lawfully for an act which was not a legal offence at the time it was committed.

The tribunal did not attempt to justify this making of retroactive laws as regards 'crimes against humanity' and 'criminal organizations'. It confined itself to trying to justify the invention of the 'crime' of 'planning and waging aggressive war' and to trying to justify the provision in Article 6 of the Charter, that 'crimes against peace' 'are crimes coming within the jurisdiction of the tribunal'.

The tribunal stated that the principle according to which criminal laws should not apply retrospectively was

161

a principle of justice, but that the principle could not restrict the legislative powers of the victors in Germany. It stated that in any event the principle ought not to apply to the accused. That is to say, the tribunal expressly discarded any pretence that the Trial was an act of justice. Nevertheless, a cardinal principle of international law was being flouted, and you would think that this alone was enough to invalidate the claim that the proceedings were in accordance with law. Yet the tribunal proceeded to contend that it was administering international law.

It contended that the Pact of Paris had made resort to war 'illegal' and 'a crime' in international law. That was to pretend that the Pact was a statute of international legislative effect, whereas really the Pact was not even an agreement on the part of the powers that signed it to avoid going to war; for the various great powers had signed it with reservations, and the reservations nullified the renunciation of the resort to war.

The tribunal then sought to justify two things. First, its own existence. Secondly, that, for the alleged violation of an agreement entered into by a number of international governments, individuals had been brought before it. To this end it drew a false analogy between the absence from the Hague Rules of any provision for setting up courts to try war crimes with a like absence from the text of the Pact of Paris of any provision for the setting up of such a court as itself. It then drew another false analogy between trials of spies and the Nuremberg Trial.

The tribunal in its Judgement used the word 'aggression' freely, not to say recklessly, alleging, for instance, that the incorporation of Austria in Greater Germany had been an act of 'aggression', even though that incorporation had been recommended in behalf of at least one of the victorious powers responsible for the present prosecution.

The truth is that the tribunal, in using the phrases 'illegal in international law' and 'crime in international law', was perpetrating an abuse of words. It misrepresented both the nature of international law and the range of applicability of that law. For the words 'international law' or 'law of nations' cannot accurately be made to do more than designate a body of rules, from which it is impossible to derive authority for the Nuremberg proceedings. The rules do not and could not authorize a state, or group of states, to invent laws for the past, and then to institute an *ad hoc* court which finds former members of another national government, military commanders in the service of that government, and certain individuals formerly in important positions under that government, guilty of having transgressed those invented laws, and, at its own discretion, sends some to death and consigns others to prison. On the contrary, the making of laws for the past is something that the rules forbid. On the contrary, the rules require that no state shall put citizens of another state on trial for alleged international offences without the previous consent of that other state. Above all, the rules are of such a nature that, before they could include a code of criminal law—as it was pretended in the Charter that they already did— this nature would have to be radically transformed.

IN THE PRECEDING PAGES I HAVE SET FORTH the evidence in support of the truth of three short statements about the Trial of the former German leaders before the international military tribunal at Nuremberg in 1945 and 1946, and, to some extent, about all the other proceedings taken by the victors against Germans termed 'war criminals', 'organizers', 'accomplices', or members of allegedly 'criminal organizations' no longer existing. That evidence I have set forth as well as I have been able to, and although it might no doubt have been set forth better, I submit that the three statements are in any event incontrovertible. They are:

1. The principal charge preferred against the accused —the charge of 'planning and waging aggressive war' and of responsibility for 'crimes against peace'—was a charge impossible to substantiate. On the first part of the charge, eight of the accused were pronounced guilty, and on the second part, twelve.

2. The other main charges—the charge of responsibility for 'war crimes' and the charge of responsibility for 'crimes against humanity', both of which, I suggest, might have been included in the Indictment so as to make the acts alleged in the first charge appear more heinous—concerned acts of various kinds, and acts of all those kinds had been committed or were being committed by or in behalf of the victors and prosecutors, and, as only Germans were indicted, the elementary principle of justice that all men are equal before the law was not observed. On each of those two charges sixteen of the accused were pronounced guilty.

3. No authority for constituting the tribunal or for holding the Trial was to be obtained from international law.

If I were to go on to inquire into the other trials held by the three western occupying powers independently in each of their areas of occupation, we should find that in the holding of those trials also elementary principles of justice were ignored, sometimes to the point of absurdity. Let it suffice for me to mention three instances.

Certain of the so-called 'major war criminals' named in the Indictment did not appear in court at Nuremberg.

One was Gustav Krupp von Bohlen und Halbach, the aged owner of the Krupps works at Essen, and he was accused on all four counts. Incidentally, he was described in the Indictment as having been head of the firm from 1922 to 1945, whereas in fact he had retired in 1943. At the time of the Trial he was too old and infirm to be put into the dock. His absence did not satisfy the chief American prosecutor, Mr. Justice Robert H. Jackson. On 12 November 1945, eight days before the Trial actually began, Mr. Jackson applied to the tribunal for Gustav Krupp's place in the dock to be taken by his son, Alfred Krupp. 'I prefer', he said, 'to have a live Krupp on the stand.' The application had the support of both the French and Russian chief prosecutors.

The British prosecutor opposed it, however. The Trial, he said, was 'not a game in which you can play one member of a team as substitute for another'. The tribunal rejected the application.

But in the United States cricket is played only at Philadelphia and on Staten Island, and the Americans did not sufficiently appreciate the weight of the English objection. Thwarted in their attempt to put Alfred Krupp into the dock before the international military tribunal, they had but to bide their time and they were able to put him into the dock before exclusively American judges. For the first, so-called 'international' tribunal was but one court to sit at Nuremberg. It was succeeded by purely American courts. Before one of these, at which Judge H. C. Anderson presided, Alfred Krupp was indicted two years later, on 17 November 1947, and sentenced at the end of July 1948. With him then were eleven other accused, either directors of Krupps or heads of departments, and all were tried on a charge of having been 'organizers' or 'accomplices'. With their fate, or with that of Alfred Krupp himself, I am not concerned. I wish simply to notice that at this trial the defence, in entering

a plea of 'Not guilty', pointed out that the indictment—
the work of Brigadier-General Telford Taylor, U.S.
army—contained references to events as far back as 1814!

In the British zone, notwithstanding that, as I have
pointed out, the term 'war crime' is a technical one with
a restricted military and legal meaning, almost anything
could constitute a 'war crime'. For instance, one German
tried as a so-called 'war criminal' was a doctor, and the
'war crime' of which he was accused amounted to no
more than obstructiveness. The hospital of which he had
had charge before the war and of which he continued
to have charge during the war was allotted to British
prisoners of war. He had refused to forward to higher
authority various communications from the senior British
army surgeon. Also, in how many trials held in the British
zone did the judge consult the chief witness for the prosecution the night before regarding the sentence to be
inflicted? 'What do we give this chap to-morrow? Fifteen
years? Will that be enough?'

As for trials in the American zone, I have already told
you[1] of the German protests to which they gave rise in
the spring and summer of 1948. Pastor Martin Niemöller
and Dr. Theophil Wurm, provincial bishop of Württemberg-Baden, and later Cardinal Frings and Monsignor
Neuhauesler, were among German religious leaders who
protested. Mr. Robert M. W. Kempner, assistant chief
prosecutor in the American trials held at Nuremberg,
replied to Dr. Wurm, but did not as much as attempt to
refute the complaints. He wrote:

It is perfectly clear that those who on whatever ground seek
to discredit the trials of war criminals are enemies of the German people and are destroying all our present hopes of a peaceful and prosperous Europe.

[1]Pp. 89 above.

A little earlier Mr. Charles M. LaFollette, director of United States military government in Württemberg-Baden, had addressed a congress of German jurists at Munich in the same strain. In a letter to German bishops, the text of which was made public at the end of June 1948, the United States military governor, General Lucius Clay himself, deplored the protests. Dr. Wurm, however, did not feel that these various replies set anything right. He stood his ground. In a letter to Mr. Kempner, he wrote:[1]

I have been greatly impressed by documents from which it was evident that in preparing the case for the prosecution in these trials, which have often ended with a sentence of death, criminal methods and abominable tortures were employed in order to extort testimony and confessions.

As I quote those episcopal words, I also have before me documents similar to those which impressed Dr. Wurm. In view of them, I do not understand what General Clay could have meant when, in his letter to the bishops, he referred to 'unconfirmed reports'. Plenty of evidence was available for him had he wanted to see it.

You will hardly quarrel with me when I say that in general the independent trials before British or American courts in Germany were dominated by a desire to secure convictions. So, I think I may say, were those before French courts. Of the proceedings of the great Trial, before the international military tribunal, it was said at the time that the presiding judge, who was English, controlled them in the best spirit of the English bench. The verdict of the tribunal included, moreover, three acquittals. Nevertheless, the provisions of the Charter, from which the tribunal obtained its jurisdiction, and the reasoning of much of the tribunal's Judgement, are

[1] *Der evangelische Sonntagsbote* (Kassel), 27 June 1948.

enough to show that the great Trial too was dominated by a desire to secure convictions. The observance of justice was subordinated to the infliction of penalties. This necessarily affects the validity of the title which the western victors wished the Trial and trials to yield to them.

I began by reminding you that the western victors invaded Germany in a punitive mood, and that everything which, following the German surrender, they decreed should be done to the German people was decreed and was done as the meting out of due retribution. Occupation, summary annexations of territory, deportations from east to west, the levy of reparations (which included the dismantling of factories and the retention of prisoners of war), and the depression of the standard of living—all that had been decreed and was carried out as if it were the infliction of a penalty on some colonial tribe that had been guilty of rebellion. In order to adopt this retributive treatment of the vanquished, the western victors, and especially the United States, felt the need of a title. The title was the 'war guilt' of the vanquished. The vanquished were to be understood to have caused the war. And the title was not, as in 1919, to be conveyed to the western victors by means of a mere assertion made in a treaty. It was to be triumphantly demonstrated in a Trial and in trials. After 1919 the 'war guilt' had been disputed. The title had been called in question. This time the intention was that it should be made indisputable. It was going to be placed beyond challenge. Yet, now that we have looked into the matter, it becomes clear that the Trial and trials were themselves but a way of dealing out retribution. That is to say, the title of the western victors to mete out retribution to the German people was not only self-conferred; it was also delivered by means of an undertaking of which the primary purpose was punitive. The western victors obtained their title to treat the vanquished as they did by thus treating them.

All over Europe the withdrawal of the German armies in 1944 and 1945, or—in Rumania, Hungary, and Bulgaria—the arrival of the Russian armies, was followed by wholesale imprisonments, and in due course there were trials and executions. According to the British under-secretary for war, speaking in the House of Commons,[1] the citizen of an allied state who might be prosecuted by the authorities of that state on account of his activities during the war was a 'quisling'. There were very many 'quislings'. The 'persecution, repression, and [judicial] murder of political opponents' was being discovered to be a 'war crime' or a 'crime against humanity' when carried out by German National Socialists. Simultaneously all over Europe governments set up after 'liberation' were making it a virtue to perpetrate that same 'crime'. 'Genocide' was in full swing. All over Europe 'quislings' were put on trial. In those trials also the ruling anxiety was not that no innocent person should suffer. The ruling anxiety was to obtain convictions.

Even here in England there was an apparent determination to ensure the punishment of William Joyce, the Irishman born in New York who had been Germany's principal broadcaster in English. A civilian amenable to trial solely before a British municipal court, he was kept in custody on the Continent without having been charged till the royal assent had been given to an Act under which he could thereupon be convicted on the evidence of a single uncorroborated witness. Furthermore, a second indictment was prepared under the Treason Act of 1940 and held in readiness to use against him had the first failed. All that had about it an air of 'We'll get him somehow'. There was, too, the curious statement made

[1]Hansard, 4 February 1946.

by Miss Rebecca West in the course of a vivid account of the Trial and of the subsequent appeals which she contributed to an American weekly.[1] Joyce, she wrote, might have been reprieved had his brother, shortly before the date for the execution, not attended a meeting of followers of Sir Oswald Mosley. Does not that suggest that the procedure of justice was being made to serve political repression?

Joyce was hanged on 3 January 1946. Two years and four months later, on 5 May 1948, Lord Jowitt, lord chancellor, said in the course of an address to the House of Lords:

I look forward to the day when, at long last, the trials of political prisoners in Europe can come to an end. I think that the indefinite prolongation of these trials is no longer performing a useful purpose. Justice, if spread over too long a period, begins to look like vengeance.

The lord chancellor's hearers received those words with marked approval. It has to be supposed that they did not perceive their full implication. If delay can make the execution of such justice as was referred to 'look like vengeance', then it cannot very well have been other than vengeance all the time. No doubt, as the years go by, the memories of witnesses grow less trustworthy. Yet, in the popular estimation at least, delay has never been thought to make retribution unjust. We have it on poetic authority that the mills of God himself grind slowly; but also that they grind sure. And as it is of the essence of what used to be called the transpontine melodrama, as of the penny dreadful, that the villain must receive his deserts in the end, so it is likewise of that essence that he shall not receive them till the end. The mere lapse of time neither lessens nor increases guilt. The guilt of Warren Hastings

[1] *The New Yorker.*

was as great and as little when the House of Commons stood to receive him in 1813 as when he was impeached twenty-six years before. But, in the words of Macaulay, 'The nation had now forgotten his faults, and remembered only his services.' The passage of time, although it cannot lessen guilt, does mellow vindictiveness. And the implication of Lord Jowitt's words was that in 1948 the English were not as vindictive as they had been in 1945. In parts of the Continent, where rancour was still unsated, malignity continued relentless. Yet, even in Czecho-Slovakia, the people's courts and the courts of honour had gone out of business a whole year before Lord Jowitt spoke, whereas at the time he spoke trials of vanquished by victors in Germany and in Japan were still going on.

It cannot be seriously pretended that those trials, whether of so-called 'war criminals', of 'organizers' or 'accomplices', or of members of former 'organizations' pronounced to have been 'criminal', were not political trials exactly as the trials of so-called 'quislings' were. It cannot be seriously pretended that the eagerness with which the prosecutions were undertaken and the pertinacity with which they were pursued did not derive from a spirit of revenge. For although the foe was now prostrate, he had come near to triumph, and especially in the countries which he had occupied on the Continent, the people who were borne aloft by his downfall were the very people he in his triumph would have kept at arm's length from power.

But nobody among the victorious peoples of the West wished to be thought nakedly revengeful. Still less did any one want to admit to himself that he was being impelled to demand the trials by a desire for vicarious vengeance. The influence of twenty centuries of a Christian tradition was still too strong to allow that. Instead there was the self-deception that the clamour for the punishment of Germans was inspired, not by a desire for vengeance, but by a desire for justice. As there had certainly been guilt, it was tempting to imagine that the guilt was wholly and exclusively German. On the strength of a wealth of atrocity stories, of the reports of the condition of concentration camps, and of all sorts of fact and rumour, it was easy to feel that justice was called for and that justice could be done.

There must often have been the same self-deception when a man was lynched. In California in the old days, when courts of law were few and far between, it was common to lynch desperadoes and to imagine that, as the victims had usually done that of which they were accused and for which they were executed, lynching was justice. But that was a self-deception none the less. Lynching cannot be justice on account of those very features in which the Nuremberg Trial was akin to lynching. A court is constituted, even if it is self-constituted. The accused is invited to try to exculpate himself, even though he will not be heeded. Usually, too, the delusion of righteousness is strong in the executioner-judges. But the guilt of the apprehended person or persons is presumed in advance, the judges have no properly constituted body of law to administer, they do not observe the rules of evidence, and the sentence pronounced is arbitrary. Hence lynching is never justice. And the Nuremberg Trial was not justice.

We can understand how natural it was for the unreasoning and warm-hearted multitude in the victorious West to fall into the self-deception that vengeance could also be justice. It is more difficult to understand how their rulers and governors were able to fancy that the prosecution and punishment of so-called 'war criminals' would be an undertaking that contributed to the future stability of peace. That self-deception was, you would have thought, too transparent. As the French Protestant

172

pastor, Jacques Ellul, wrote in a weekly paper in the week following the delivery of the sentences:[1]

We did not wreak vengeance: that would have made us wicked! But we manufactured a special and entirely novel law designed to enable us to sentence to death.

How could it have been imagined that, first the Germans, and then the world, would not realize this?

Already in November 1947 a German lecturer at Heidelberg was predicting that in Germany every detail of the Trial, and details of some of the later trials too, would become the topic of interminable discussion down the years, and that the Trial was destined to engender a German literature as vast as that provoked by Article 231 of the Treaty of Versailles. After all, the prediction was not surprising. The circumstances of the Trial, far from putting it beyond challenge, simply invited challenge. But what will be the sequel?

The western victors were harking back to the ferocious after-war exactions of the victorious Greeks and Romans. Indeed, they were being more obstinately vindictive than Augustus, who is credited with having taken to heart the precept of Aeneas:

Parcere subiectis et debellare superbos.

Earlier in this century the international conferences held at The Hague had seemed to reflect a more reasonable international temper. After the Boer War the victors shook hands with the vanquished. Thanks to the mediation of Theodore Roosevelt, the Russo-Japanese war was brought to a conclusion which both sides could feel to be honourable. That was in accordance with a very old tradition, deeply rooted in the European past. The ancient Greek cosmogonies took it for granted that hos-

[1] *Réforme* (Paris), 12 October 1946.

tility between belligerents would end with the end of hostilities. The gods of the Greek mythology might go to war. Once the fighting was over, they all returned to their seats on Olympus, victors and vanquished sitting down together again. There were no grudges. There was no ill-will. Once Asklepios had been struck down by Zeus, he nevertheless remained a tutelary god. Although Prometheus and Kronos were both the foes of Zeus, one made an end in heaven and was brought there by Herakles; the other went to reign over the Isles of the Blessed. Hostility and hostilities had the same end.

As the Greeks grew more 'civilized' and more and more determined to achieve internecine destruction, that old tradition was discarded. During the Peloponnesian War there were horrible reprisals and acts of vengeance. Later there was the savage razing of the town of Thebes. Then, on the death of Alexander the Great, the Athenians rose in revolt, and the generals to whom Alexander bequeathed his empire, after they had quelled them, took punitive measures. Three of the Athenian leaders, Aristonicus, Himeraeus, and Hyperides, were caught and put to death. But the greatest leader, Demosthenes, escaped. He fled to the Island of Calauria. There are few more moving pages in Plutarch than those which describe how he was pursued and what happened when he was overtaken. Archias, the hunter of fugitives and desecrator of sanctuaries, went after Demosthenes to Calauria. Archias intended if possible to entice him, if necessary to force him, to Antipater's camp, so that there he might meet the fate of a 'major war criminal'. But Demosthenes foiled Archias and perished honourably by his own hand. Demosthenes cheated the executioner. I do not have to tell you that the sympathies of all after-generations have been, not with Antipater and Archias, but with Demosthenes. Will our sons and grandsons see Goering attain the apotheosis of national martyrdom? Such a sequel was invited. For, like Demosthenes, Goering cheated the executioner, and on the eve of being put to death in cold blood by the enemies of his country, he died by his own hand. In the course of time Germans may well forget that he had helped to bring ignominy, disaster, and ruin upon them, and his end alone will be remembered.

You will perhaps ask: 'But were not the so-called "major war criminals" guilty, and did not their guilt matter more than anything else?' The answer to that question had already been delivered down the centuries by the moral sense of civilized mankind. And there lies one dreadful significance of the great Nuremberg Trial.

That moral sense had long held it better for the guilty to escape punishment than for the innocent to suffer and for courts of justice to become unjust. The Nuremberg Trial, and not the Nuremberg Trial alone, but also the other trials of individuals among the vanquished at the hands of the victors, and, furthermore, the numerous political trials of so-called 'quislings', reflected an old notion of the duty of a court of law which the Continent of Europe discarded at the French Revolution and England never knew.

To make clear what I mean, it is necessary to go back to the thirteenth century when the Church set up the Inquisition on the Continent. In some countries the activities of the Inquisition were restricted, in others they were very far-reaching. But throughout the Continent the procedure adopted in ecclesiastical courts was to serve as a model, and under their influence secular courts too became inquisitorial. The suppression of the Albigensian heresy had been entrusted to the Dominicans, and in view of their success in extirpating it, they were given charge of the prosecution of heretics in general. According to Maitland, the great historian of English law:[1]

---

[1] Sir Frederick Pollock and F. W. Maitland, *The History of English Law before the Time of Edward I* (2nd ed.), II, 557.

The procedure by way of inquisition soon assumed all its worst characteristics. Every safeguard of innocence was abolished or disregarded; torture was freely used. Everything seems to be done to secure a conviction. This procedure, inquisitory and secret, gradually forced its way into the temporal courts; we may almost say that the common law of Europe adopted it.

But while the Inquisition was established on the Continent, it never gained a footing in England, and hence, as Maitland says, 'England at the critical moment . . . escaped the taint of the *inquisitio haereticae pravitatis*'.

The escape [Maitland says][1] was narrow. . . . Happily, however, the reforms of Henry II were effected before the days of Innocent III. Our new procedure seemed to hesitate for a while at the meeting of two roads. A small external impulse might have sent it down the too easy path which the church chose and which led to the everlasting bonfire. All that was necessary was that the sworn declarations of the hundredors should be treated as testimony. As regards some matters of small importance this was done. . . . But where the imputation is grave, the words of the jurors are treated not as testimony but as mere accusation. . . .

The canonists were evolving a law, and a rigorous law, of evidence. 'Full proof' consists of the accordant testimony of two unexceptionable witnesses who have themselves seen the crime committed. . . . Such proof was rarely to be had, more especially as large classes of mankind were incapable of testifying. One must eke out a 'half proof' by the confession of the accused, and to obtain this torture is used. Luckily for England neither the stringent rules of legal proof nor the cruel and stupid subterfuge became endemic here. Whether we may ascribe to our ancestors any unusual degree of humanity or enlightenment is doubtful. . . . But our ancestors had not been corrupted by the persecution of heretics. Foreign criminalists in the middle ages and in later times are for ever dwelling on the weakness of the law, on the difficulty of obtaining convictions unless the

[1]Op. cit., II, 657-60.

state takes to itself every advantage in its struggles with the prisoner. Of this we hear little in England, though we can see that an enormous quantity of crime went unpunished.

Maitland mentions how in one visitation to Gloucester in the year 1221 the justices heard of three hundred and thirty acts of homicide, but, as a result of the visitation, only one man was mutilated and fourteen men were hanged.

Suppose you to ask me if the guilt of the accused did not make it of no account that the charge of 'crimes against peace' was a charge impossible to substantiate, of no account that the charges of 'war crimes' and of 'crimes against humanity' were one-sided, of no account that much of the reasoning of the tribunal, in its Judgement, was questionable, and of no account that the holding of the Trial was pretended legal only by means of a gross distortion of the nature of international law. The answer is that in England in the middle ages 'an enormous quantity of crime went unpunished', but that both innocence and justice were protected, and for that protection the escape of the guilty did not seem too high a price to pay. The sentiment of civilized mankind, whenever it has not been swayed by passion or warped by self-interest, has been unanimous in insisting that it is better for ninety and nine guilty persons to escape sentence than for one innocent to be convicted.

Of that moment when English procedure narrowly escaped taking the same road as procedure on the Continent, Maitland says:[1] 'It was a critical moment in English legal history, and therefore in the innermost history of our land and race.' Another critical moment —this time in the legal history of Europe—was reached in the eighteenth century, when, on the eve of the French Revolution,

[1]Op. cit., II, 673.

French philosphers and jurists rebelled against [the inquisitory and secret procedure inherited from the Inquisition] and looked about them for an accusatory, contradictory, public procedure, a procedure which knew no torture.[1]

And, as Maitland says, 'they looked to ancient Rome and modern England'.

Now in the twentieth century it seems as if a third critical moment had been reached in legal history. Judicial procedure is to turn its back on English tradition and custom, that tradition and custom which spread to the Continent at the French Revolution. In the political trials that followed the war in so many countries of the Continent, the old anxiety revived to obtain convictions at all costs. In trials of Germans before courts set up by the western victors in the territories of their occupation, both 'confessions' and evidence were sometimes obtained by torture. The plea that an act was done in obedience to superior orders was not accepted. Sentence was sometimes determined in advance. In the Trial of the so-called 'major war criminals' at Nuremberg there may have been no torture and no doubt witnesses testified freely, although it is not insignificant that a number failed to appear in person. But in that Trial especially the desire to punish predominated over the desire to do justice. There were altogether thirty-six convictions on three charges alleging acts which could only have been performed, if they were performed, before they were made 'crimes', and those 'crimes' were hitherto unknown to law. The accused were indicted, tried, and condemned under an *ad hoc* 'law' invented by the prosecution. 'We did not wreak vengeance: that would have made us wicked! But we manufactured a special and entirely novel law designed to enable us to sentence to death.'

[1]Op. cit., II, 657.

For a new heresy hunt the old forms of persecution were resuscitated.

At Westminster in the middle ages judicial decency and fairness were being secured for civilized men all the way down to our own time. As Maitland says, in the concluding words of his great history,

> Those few men who were gathered at Westminster round Pateshull and Raleigh and Bracton were penning writs that would run in the name of kingless commonwealths on the other shore of the Atlantic Ocean; they were making right and wrong for us and for our children.

But for us that right and wrong have not been good enough, and from one kingless commonwealth on the other side of the Atlantic Ocean men have come to Europe in order to impose on Europeans another right and wrong. Once again a critical moment has been reached in the legal history of Europe, and therefore in the innermost history of western man. All over the Continent courts have harked back to the worst forms of procedure in use during the middle ages. At the beginning of this century the tide seemed to be flowing all the other way. But with the advent of totalitarian states the tide turned and ebbed. It was in National Socialist Germany and in Communist Russia that once again every safeguard of innocence was abolished or disregarded, and torture was freely used. In fact, in the institution and conduct of the post-war trials of individuals among the vanquished, the western victors over Germany came to resemble that which they fought the war to destroy. Having won a great war in a cause which the world was all ready to believe noble, they hastened to ruin that cause. 'To speak of ourselves as a Christian society, in contrast to that of Germany or Russia, is an abuse of terms', Mr. T. S. Eliot wrote in 1939.[1] 'We conceal from ourselves the similarity of our society to those which we execrate.' The similarity to which he referred the war did but increase, and the concealment of it from ourselves was made more difficult. Jekyll and Hyde were out-jekylled, and we have a horror exceeding any horror of the Elizabethan drama. For St. George slew the dragon only to find that it was the dragon's features which confronted him when he beheld his natural face in a glass.

That is bad enough. But it is not all.

The political trials which followed the war in many countries of the Continent were at least trials in which the accused were judged and convicted at the behest of their own government. But the Nuremberg Trial and all the other trials of individuals among the vanquished at the hands of the victors were trials in which the accused were judged and convicted by foreigners. The popular pretext for them was summed up in the words: '*We* had to punish *them*.' Of the whole war, not conspicuous for nobility of feeling, that assertion was surely the supreme vulgarity!

Why 'them'? Why not ourselves? And why *had* 'we'? The only answer returned to those questions was that 'they' were bad, and 'we' were good. 'We'—namely, the western victors—were solely concerned for law and order, and it was law and order that we wished to vindicate in punishing them. 'We' triumphed, not because we were the stronger and the more numerous, but because 'we' had right on our side. That is to say, the other side was wrong, and consequently wicked. Yet, if pressed, 'we' would have had to admit that the only ground for the belief that right was on the winning side was that it was our side.

[1] *The Idea of a Christian Society.*

But the Trial and the trials were undertaken, you may say, in obedience to a conviction stronger and less ingenuous than that belief. It was the conviction that the law of nations had been transgressed, and that, as transgressions of law inside each country are punished, so transgressions of the law of nations ought to be punished likewise. The conviction was only in another form the belief that right was on the winning side because it was 'our' side.

The delusion that international law needed only a court and sentences in order to become criminal law sprang from a radical misunderstanding both of the nature of international law and of the situation of independent sovereign states. There was a fatal confusion of force and right, and a lamentable obliviousness to the indispensable requisites of international morality.

Some historians declare that in early civilized societies, such as the Roman republic, retroactive criminal laws had to be devised because transgressions occurred which the drafting of the laws already in force did not foresee. On an analogy with that practice, it was contended that the promulgation of the Charter of 8 August 1945 and the setting up of the international military tribunal were designed to deal with transgressions of international law for which no judicial procedure had hitherto been provided. Apparently the persons who put forward the contention never paused to notice that such acts as were now alleged to be transgressions of international law had been going on throughout recorded time. They never paused to wonder why, if the invention of an international criminal justice was so easy, it had not been invented before.

There was, indeed, a very good reason. When retroactive laws were made by the Roman republic, they were made by a government; that is to say, the legislative authority was properly qualified to make laws by its relation to the governed. On that account there can be no analogy between the gradual elaboration of criminal law in an early society and the outrages in international behaviour perpetrated in 1945 and 1946 by means of the Charter and of the Trial before the international military tribunal. The victors had received the unconditional surrender of the vanquished, and, having denied to the vanquished a government of their own, they were themselves, as regards the vanquished, in a relation of government to the governed. But that relation could obviously only hold concerning the current discharge of *national* government and administration, whereas the Charter and the Trial were concerned with the *international* conduct of the vanquished. In the international domain, there was, and there could be, no relation of government to governed. In that domain the victors were simply a coalition of states that went through the motions of legislating for and judging the governments and leaders of another state like themselves. Their legal and moral status was no more than that of a gang of lynchers dealing with a victim. They were able to do what they did as lynchers are able to lynch. That is to say, they were the stronger. Their only sanction was force; and, although law needs force in order to ensure its respect, it is in no sense identical with force. At Nuremberg the victors were but John Bull, Jonathan, Alphonse, and Uncle Bruin masquerading as the Ku Klux Klan.

It was pointed out by the defence that the charter of the United Nations contained no condemnation of 'aggressive war', and that point the tribunal ignored. It is important to see that even had the Nuremberg Charter been drawn up and promulgated and the Trial held at the bidding of the United Nations, the proceeding would still have had no legal and moral authority. The United

Nations could no more have had a legal and moral status to administer and to enforce an international criminal 'law' than a coalition of four victorious states had. For the United Nations itself is simply a larger coalition of independent sovereign states. And so long as independent sovereign states are but states, they can produce no legal or moral authority for the exercise, either singly or as a coalition, of legislative and executive powers outside their respective territories. Above each independent sovereign state there is no higher power, only God.

The one terrestrial body there could be with legal and moral authority to have promulgated the Charter and to have held the Trial is a government above individual states. That is to say, it could only be a super-government, the government of a world state. But this is a moral world, and the essential condition of morality in international behaviour is that there shall be no world state. For a single government of the whole world could only endure if it were omnipotent. It could not be merely supernational. It would have to abolish nationality. It would have to be invested with the power to interfere in the internal affairs of each of the various national states which had delegated to it their own sovereignty. The United States of North America began in 1781 as a confederation. The federal government, in its exercise of power over the states of the union, was restricted to dealing with the various state governments. It had no power over the citizens of those states as individuals. That is why the confederation was a failure. Unless nationalities were abolished, nothing could make a world government effective. It would be restricted to expressing the same pious hopes that were contained in the Pact of Paris. If, however, a world government did have the power to rule the whole world, there could be no limit to that power, and it would be a tyranny.

183

That is why all talk of a world state, all talk of an international police force, all talk of an international criminal justice, is pernicious and immoral.

The rules termed collectively the law of nations are essentially moral rules. Any attempt to transform them into a criminal law could but result in their falling into total desuetude. International law can grow and has grown. That is not in dispute. But it cannot suddenly apply to a new sphere of human affairs. It could only be made to include an international criminal code by a world state, and to a world state empowered to enforce the code, the code would be superfluous. Under a genuine world government nothing would be international. Nationalities would have to be all absorbed in one worldwide nation. The world government would inevitably be led to behave in utter disregard of morality. This would happen owing to the removal of the two conditions that make international morality possible. On the one hand, the practice of morality needs neighbours. As no man could be moral if alone in the world, so independent sovereign states can only be moral in a community of nations. Pluralism is indispensable. On the other hand, a world state would have to be absolute if it were to endure. We do not need Acton's assurance that absolute power corrupts absolutely. It is a truism. As Montesquieu points out in *L'Esprit des Lois*, the one effective limitation on power is rival power. It is the existence of other states that puts a limit to the power that can be exercised by any single state. It is the restriction of power that leads the exercise of power to be moral.

It follows that the law of nations can never have the sanctions which sovereignty confers on positive or municipal law. International law cannot become criminal law. No sovereign state is to be commanded to respect the needs and sentiments of other sovereign states. Each state has a duty to respect those needs and sentiments, but the duty is a purely moral one.

As each state has the moral duty to respect the human person, the family, and the associations and groups that are lawfully formed within itself, so in the international community each state has the moral duty to respect the sovereignty and independence of other states by accepting limitations on the exercise of its own sovereign power.

It has the duty to recognize where damage has been unjustly inflicted on another state and the duty to repair that damage. The recognition can only be voluntary, and the amount of the damage can only be assessed as a result of mutual agreement. This comes about through arbitration. Perhaps the most famous and instructive instance is that of the damage done by the ships Alabama, Shenandoah, and Florida, which, having been built in British shipyards, were allowed to go out of British ports during the American civil war in violation of neutrality. Much damage ensued, but it required years to arrive at a settlement. It was only in September 1872 that referees—who included a representative of Britain as well as a representative of the United States—awarded the United States $15½ million in compensation, and Britain accepted the award.

The essence of such a settlement is that it shall be arrived at by mutual consent. Where the guilty party is not allowed to give its free consent, we are in the realm of lawless force. It is solely by the exercise of lawless force that victors in a war can seize individuals among the vanquished once the vanquished have been disarmed, and, for offences alleged to have been committed against the victors themselves or their nationals, in the course of hostilities, proceed to try and to punish them. That cannot be lawful. It is merely to carry on war after the fighting has ended. It is merely to carry on a coward's war.

In 1919 the western victors wished to levy reparations

on the vanquished, and they felt that they must have a title to do so. This title they conferred on themselves by means of an assertion of 'war guilt' which they inserted in their peace treaty. A second war having broken out in 1939, the same western victors assumed that its cause must again lie in the 'war guilt' of the vanquished. They supposed that there had been only one error after 1918: the punishment inflicted on the vanquished was not sufficiently severe. In order to inflict even more drastic punishment this time, they again felt the need of a title. It was the same title, namely, the 'war guilt' of the vanquished. But this time they wished to render it, as they must have supposed, unchallengeable. They delivered it to themselves by means of the verdict of a tribunal.

That verdict was, however, worthless. To some extent the holding of the Trial at which it was rendered had been dictated by a desire for vengeance. In addition, the penalties upon individuals which the tribunal inflicted as a result of the verdict were as much punishment of the vanquished as any of the more general punitive treatment which the verdict was held to warrant. That is to say, the conveyance of the title was itself of a kind with that which it was held to render permissible.

Furthermore, the prosecution and punishment of individuals among the vanquished at the hands of the victors after the war had ended were an undertaking fraught with grave menace for the future of civil manners. The prosecution and punishment were carried out according to a totalitarian notion of justice which neither England nor 'kingless commonwealths on the other shore of the Atlantic Ocean' had ever known, and which the Continent of Europe had discarded at the French Revolution. In the principal Trial there was the sinister pretension to administer international law. That meant in effect that this Trial was an attempt to degrade the law of nations from a set of moral rules to a criminal code, an

186

attempt which, if it could ever succeed, would abolish the law of nations altogether.

Against those grave judicial and moral abuses, can there be set anything that was achieved for the cause of peace? On the contrary, it now seems more probable than in my beginning that nothing is to be gained after a war by the punishment of the vanquished by the victors, even if the vanquished have been to blame for the war itself. It now seems more probable than ever that for victors to assert after a war the 'war guilt' of the vanquished serves but to disguise the real sources of international disturbance.

Possibly it is because the western victors in 1919 did not recognize the moral basis of international relations that war returned to Europe and to the world in 1939. Possibly it is because the western victors again in 1945 did not recognize the moral basis of those relations that the world was treated to the spectacle of victors' justice, and one more great war had ended without leading men's feet into the way of peace.